AFTER

STORIES ABOUT LOSS &
WHAT COMES NEXT

AFTER

edited by

MELISSA FOURNIER
DANIEL W. STEWART

EST'D 2018
BARNWOOD BOOKS
TRAVERSE CITY, MICHIGAN

BARNWOOD BOOKS is a subsidiary of
History By Design
P.O. Box 1224
Traverse City, Michigan 49685
HistoryByDesign.net

Book design by Daniel Stewart | *daniel@historybydesign.net*

On the cover: "Shadow of Person on Water during Daytime" by Skitterphoto, used under a Creative Commons license.

Greta Bolger's poems were previously published in *Silver Birch Press* (Dec 2015) and *Eclectica* (Jan/Feb 2018).

ISBN: 978-1-949285-03-1

Printed and bound in the United States of America.

Contents

Melissa Fournier

Introduction

Fracture is a sudden rupture in the skin of the afternoon. A crack, a tear, a rending apart of what once was whole. A violence.
—Arianne Zwartjes, *Detailing Trauma: A Poetic Anatomy*

I sat perched on the railroad ties that bordered my mother's flowerbeds at the edge of our driveway, squinting at the sun's gleam off the silver U-Haul, watching my father walk back and forth from garage to truck, truck to garage, loading his belongings. I was three years old. The meaning of the word divorce, a word I mispronounced as *diborce*, was unfolding before me. My first fracture.

When I was twelve, I stood in the same driveway under a chilly autumn rain, my face buried in the folds of my father's nylon jacket. His car ran idle, blowing exhaust into the air as I said good-bye. "We don't say good-bye," he insisted, "we say see you later." This was the night before he moved fourteen hundred miles away with his wife and step-daughter. Six months later, he was diagnosed with lung cancer.

I saw him one more time before he died. During that visit, he looked into my almost-thirteen year old eyes and asked me, "Do I look like I'm going to live or die?"

"You'll live," I said. "You'll live."

But I knew this was true only in the eternal sense, and after he died, I did what many bereaved teen-agers do—I disconnected from the pain of grief, disconnected from repeated fracture. I told myself I didn't see him much anyway and I poured myself into my books and studies.

Six months after my father's death, my mother picked me up from school with the news that my cousin, a center for Michigan State's football team and the oldest in the line of fourteen cousins, died of suicide in a park by his house. It was fifteen days before his twenty-fifth birthday. His death became a turning point in our extended family. A sense of family pride was replaced by darkness and shame; distance and isolation replaced closeness and connection. Gatherings became heavy and awkward, and eventually dwindled to funerals and weddings, always with some of us missing, always with an unacknowledged void.

The losses for my immediate family continued for another three years, so many that we began to see our circle as cursed—illnesses, asphyxiation, electrocution, sudden heart attacks—friends young and old who mattered to us.

I essentially disconnected from all of them until January 28th, 1986, when my teacher clicked on the television in my eleventh grade chemistry class. The Space Shuttle Challenger exploded—and I imploded. I watched the disaster footage over and over again, questioned God, the meaning of life, and cried for Christa McAuliffe, the teacher in space, as if she were my own mother. Disaster jokes circulated around my high school, and I outwardly chuckled in effort to conceal my inner turmoil.

I tucked this grief away, too, but became deeply interested in human psychology, family dynamics, and existential suffering. I went on to study psychology and social work in college, and made a career of counseling others.

Well into family life and my late thirties, I endured another fracture, a tearing actually, of the placenta away from the womb during my third pregnancy. This resulted in the premature birth and ultimately the death of our youngest child. A girl we named Camille Grace. A girl who lived for ninety minutes. A girl whose cold and blue body I would not let go of for twenty-six hours after her death. This fracture, this breakage, brought forth the torrent of griefs I had not reconciled. Not only did I grieve the loss of our daughter and what would never be, but the losses I'd packed away so well as a teen.

Through this process, through exploring and honoring my unreconciled (and what those in the bereavement field call *complicated*) grief, I began to see how loss and death shaped my life—how present it had been from my earliest years—and how, in a sense, my life had been drawn with the pencil of absence. I remembered my mother flittering her fingers above a globe as she explained the concept of heaven to me after our pediatrician, Dr. Schneider, died when I was four. I remembered standing at the open casket of a third grade classmate, Gina, who was laid to rest in her white First Communion dress, a dress just like the one all of the girls in my class and I wore months earlier. I remembered my grandmother wailing, "he's gone...he's gone..." as we left the cemetery at my grandfather's interment when I was nine, and I have come to understand that this compilation of experiences—this death curriculum—was necessary training for what would become my work in hospice and bereavement. Necessary training for living, even.

A few years ago, I learned of the Japanese art of *kintsugi*, in which pottery, when broken, is treated with a lacquered resin dusted with gold so the breakage is accentuated instead of hidden. The mended piece is not only *as* beautiful, but *more* beautiful with its visible history of fractures than the original. This art form, said to date back to the fifteenth century, is gaining modern resurgence in our culture of brokenness and violent fracture. The philosophy behind this form inspired me to find my own piece of kintsugi to place in my office, where I do the work of holding the stories of those who are bereaved, of those whose lives know fracture, of those who vacillate between before and after. Before the accident. Before the divorce. Before the diagnosis. After that night. After the phone call. After the death.

But I do not do this work as a kintsugi artist. I do it as one who has been broken and who has come to know the importance of allowing others to help us become whole again. I used to think I had to disguise my brokenness. I imagined that if I could make my environment as perfect as possible, if I strove for excellence within myself, and if I hid my vulnerability, my fractures would become invisible, at least to the naked eye. In the space of fracture, of breakage, out of self-protection and necessity, I folded inward. But ultimately, through grace, I found a way to unfold toward transformation. This transformation occurred by allowing myself to become vulnerable, by allowing others into the private space of my most hurt self. Others have been the gold with which I have been repaired, and in turn, we who've been made more whole become the gold for those who are newly shattered.

The pieces you will find in this book invite us to come together as companions into fracture and repair, into the space of mending. They invite us to become the gold in the resin for one another, and to see ourselves and our experiences as the material of the potter, who makes us nothing less than exquisite.

TO YOU, AND TO AFTER.

AFTER

Alison Hartman

Mending

The findings are clear:
a hairline fracture circumnavigates her heart.
A slight seepage of blood oozes a bright red
zig zag ring like a bolt of lightning
that blazed the moment he died.
They say her prognosis is good
but it's impossible to say
how long the healing will take.
Always there will be a scar,
not the kind that forms on the skin.
Scars of the heart heal differently.
Fractures of the heart knit together
in a pattern woven with love.
The deeper the love,
the deeper the seam.
Tears clean the wound.
Rest provides repair.
Breath bathes the bereaved
in a soothing salve.
The wind, the stars, the trees console,
and the ocean tides rock back and forth
in a lullaby.

Rosemarie Canfield

Pilgrim

The smell of Isaac's famous French fries—fresh cut from russet potatoes, fried to a golden brown—filled the autumn air as Steve and I rode our bikes up his long driveway. We smelled hamburgers cooking on the open fire.

This wasn't just any gathering, but a going away party for me. My son Isaac and his wife Mary had invited a few family members and friends to say good bye and wish me well on my adventure. Isaac loved to get together. As he liked to say, "It's about making memories."

Before I wanted, though, the evening was ending. Children needed to go to bed, and it was a work night for others. As the gathering diminished, Isaac gave me a big hug and asked, "You sure you want to do this?"

I leaned into his hug, "Yes, I'm sure, Isaac," I said. "Don't worry. I'll be safe."

The next morning my good friend Brenda and I were leaving to walk the Camino de Santiago. We would be starting in France and hiking 500 miles through Spain, along the network of pilgrimage trails ending in the cathedral of Santiago de Compostela, at the shrine to St. James, the first of the Apostles to be martyred.

We planned on being gone six, maybe eight weeks. I had never been gone that long from my family. We had researched, studied and physically prepared for this trip of a lifetime. It was physically and spiritually challenging, but I felt ready and embraced it all. Forward, one foot in front of the other, mile after mile, with no cell service and limited communication due to the language barrier—it was up to *me* to finish.

WE HAD SPENT THREE WEEKS ON THE TRAIL, AND THE city of Burgos would be our next stop.

The day before Burgos, rain met us the moment we stepped outside the front door of our lodging, called an *albergues*—a refuge. The rain beat against us with no letup and soaked us to the bone. The terrain was rough and unforgiving; fatigue settled in and we knew we needed rest. Both of us felt the need to stay in a hotel with hot showers and privacy, something the *albergues* seldom offered. Burgos was a welcome sight.

That night I turned off my phone in hope of a peaceful night's rest. In the morning I turned it back on. The light from it illuminated the dark morning of our hotel. Several messages began to fill my screen:

"Mom call home ASAP!" It was Abraham, my oldest son.

I couldn't dial fast enough. "Abe," I said, "what's going on?"

"Mom, you may want to come home," he said, his voice tightly controlled. "Isaac's in surgery. It's his heart. The doctor has given him a 90 percent chance—he's the top surgeon and has done this surgery successfully before."

"Is Dad there?"

For the first time I sensed tension in Abe's voice. "Yes, Mom," he said. "We're all here."

"I'm coming home."

I quickly relayed the message to Brenda. "You can finish the trail if you want," I said, "but I'm going home."

"Rose," she said, "we started together, and we'll stay together."

Within minutes we gathered the clothes we'd scattered around the room in an attempt to dry them before we hit the trail, and stuffed them into our backpacks. I ran down to the front desk. "My son is in the hospital in America," I almost shouted to the clerk. "I need a cab to get to Madrid Airport."

Brenda and I waited out in front of the hotel. The early morning air was damp from the night's rain, and it stuck to my skin. Worse, it made my lungs heavy as my heart raced, my mind filled with imaginings of what was going on back home. The feeling of being separated from my family never felt so painful. I felt every inch of the thousands of miles between us.

On our way to Madrid I stared out my side window and watched the dark morning turn to pink as the sun rose. *How could this be happening?* The landscape changed from rolling hills to villages. The traffic increased while the sun became brighter.

We had been on the road about an hour when I felt a lifting inside me, like a breath deep within me pulling out. I turned to look at Brenda. Breaking the deafening silence that surrounded us, I said, "Brenda, I think he's going to be alright."

Her response was quick and full of confidence. "Of course he is, Rose," she said. "He's young and strong. He'll be okay."

Two hours later we arrived at Madrid Airport. As I waited for the cab driver to get our things out of his trunk, minutes felt like hours. I gave him all the money I had—by his surprised look, a gross overpayment—then we both ran into the airport. I tried my phone: no signal. *Are you kidding me?* I was desperate beyond words.

At the American Airlines desk, we both pushed our charge cards across the counter. Brenda said, "We need to book a flight."

"Look," I blurted out, "I need to get home. My son is in the hospital in America and I have no cell service. I need to call my family. Please, is there some way I can call out?"

The kind ticket agent picked up the receiver of her landline phone and dialed out, allowing me to call Abraham.

"Abe?" I said into the handset.

Nothing. It sounded like he had dropped the phone.

"Abe!" I said again.

I heard only broken sentences, gasping breath, and tears that turned to deep sobbing.

"I can't understand you," I said. "Slow down. What's going on?"

Then I heard my husband's voice. He must have taken the phone from Abe.

"Steve?" I said. "Steve—what's happening?"

"We—" he began, but there was more sobbing., and then: "—lost our Isaac. He's gone, honey. He's gone."

My body collapsed. I couldn't breathe. The phone slid from the desk, landing beside me, all forming a tangled heap. I lay on the cold Madrid airport floor, banging the receiver, screaming, "No! No! You're lying to me! Get someone here that can tell me the truth. You're lying to me!" I began to weep uncontrollably.

"It's true, honey," he said. "I just kissed him goodbye."

"No—not my Isaac!" I pounded the floor.

Brenda took the receiver from me. I could hear her asking Steve what happened.

She later told me what he said to her: "Isaac's gone. Just get my wife home, Brenda. Just get her home."

Brenda and an airport attendant helped me up into a chair. I sat frozen in disbelief.

With tears in her eyes, the ticket agent slid our charge cards and tickets toward Brenda. "No fee," she said.

I looked at my ticket. It read: A DEATH IN THE FAMILY. I couldn't believe it. There must be a mistake. Not my Isaac.

What a mean thing for God to do.

WE ARRIVED AT DETROIT METRO AT MIDNIGHT. THE airport looked like a ghost town, lonely and desolate, as we made our way to be picked up. Steve met me there. We embraced, two broken, bleeding parents.

"I want to drive, Steve," I said, "and I want you to tell me everything." He handed me the keys.

Upon entering the car, Steve asked if I would like a bottle of water.

"No!" I screamed at him, banging on the steering wheel. "I want our son. I want to see Isaac."

With a broken voice he answered, "You can't, Rose. Not yet."

I leaned on the steering wheel while Steve sat in the passenger's seat, our shoulders slumped. We wept. Once we got ourselves under control, we began our four-hour journey north to our home.

We had other adult children racing to come home: driving from Texas and from New Jersey; flying from Florida. We—my husband and I and our eight other children, some with spouses and our grandchildren—would all be together for the first time in quite a while. Yet this would be our first time with this gaping hole, a hole the shape of Isaac.

Consumed with grief, unaware of the jet lag, I did not sleep. Trying to put one foot in front of the other took all the energy I had. On the morning of the day after my return, five of us—Mary, Isaac's wife; Abe and his wife; and Steve and me—made the long drive to do the unthinkable.

The funeral director greeted us, then led us all to a chilly conference room with a large wooden table surrounded by cushioned chairs. She was a kind young woman, the daughter of a long-time friend. She had even visited a few times and played at our farm with Isaac when they were children. What an ugly twist, that now she sat across from us discussing funeral arrangements for my son.

I remember little of the conversation, as the talk was between Mary and the funeral director. After all, as Isaac's wife, she would have final say.

I asked the funeral director if I could please see my son. She strongly discouraged me. I had an urge to run through that funeral home and swing each and every door open until I could find my son, grab him, and weep into his strong shoulders. I had wanted to see Isaac from the moment I heard that he had died. I wanted to tell him that I loved him. I wanted to hold him. I was his mother.

Mary's voice was soft as she answered the many difficult questions, the final one being, "Would you like us to take a fingerprint of Isaac? It's often used to make a necklace as a memory piece."

Mary hesitated, and with a puffy, tear-stained face she answered, barely audibly, "Yes. I think I might like that."

I thought, *There is no way Mary will have the strength to*

order this. She was so broken and devastated over the loss of her husband and the thought of what lay ahead. Their marriage had seemed to me like a fairytale love story, but now it lay shattered. I knew right then and there I would buy that necklace for her. I felt almost selfish wanting one for myself, too, but no one had asked me.

AT THE VISITATION, IT'S FAMILY FIRST. STEVE AND I entered with Mary. Following her were their children: Uriah, ten, tall and thoughtful; Tirzah, eight, sweet and beautiful; Shemuel, six, strong and energetic, a look-alike to his father; and Hadassah, just two, daddy's little firecracker. They had brought treasures for their dad—colored pictures, paper airplanes, love notes and a favorite doll, all to be placed in their father's casket.

There are no words for the feelings a mother has as she walks up to her son's casket. It should be me, my husband, that's the order—not this, not my son first. This sting of death was piercing my heart as I walked closer to my once-vibrant young son and friend.

The children laid their gifts around their father's lifeless body. The airplane went in his shirt pocket, with the other gifts placed gently on his body. They were ushered toward a private room, but my six-year-old grandson sat in a chair and rubbed his eyes. "I can't do this, Grandma," he said. "I can't do this. It's too hard."

I hugged him and reassured him that it was okay, until he went to join his siblings.

I stared at my son's lifeless body. I ran my hands over his bald head and down his cheek to his chest, meeting the hands that lay folded on his belly. His fingers were those of a woodsman—rough and stained. I moved his fingers, and they were not stiff. I rubbed my hand over his. I remembered when he was a little boy, how I would rub bag balm on those once-little boy hands to soften them after a hard day of working on the farm. There were scars on his hands; each tells a story of a boy becoming a man. I looked back at Isaac's face.

"What have they done to my Isaac?" I said.

Abraham, older than Isaac by two years and the best friend who had been beside him since his birth, heard me and softly answered, "Mom, they tried to save him."

With tears running down my cheeks, I leaned forward and I laid my head on Isaac's chest. "Abe," I said, "go get Dad."

In a moment Steve was by my side, with his hand on the small of my back. "What do you need, honey?"

"I want to hug Isaac. He needs a hug. I need to hug him. Help me."

The funeral director had prepared me for what it would feel like to hug my son. Steve, with the help of the funeral director, gently lifted Isaac to a seated position. I wrapped my arms around him, pulling his head into my shoulder. "God," I said, "give me my son back." *Give me a Lazarus moment*, I begged.

God didn't. Too soon, the hug had to end. They laid Isaac peacefully back down. It was the last hug I ever gave my son.

The day following the viewing, we placed our son's body in the cold October earth. His five brothers had dug his grave under the maple tree in the hay field, now turned cemetery. They lowered their brother slowly to his final resting place. We dropped white roses on his shiny cedar casket. Tears were shed, but none as sad as his two year old daughter as she stood beside her father's open grave, her tiny shoulders rising and falling as she sobbed and repeated, over and over, "I miss my daddy. I miss my daddy."

The next day would be the memorial. And two days after that would be my birthday.

My son had died five days before my 62nd birthday. Other family members had decided to celebrate, but there was not a bone in my body that wanted any kind of a party. The grandchildren helped blow out the candles. Everyone around me tried hard to embrace the celebration, eating cake and ice cream.

I went into another room and cried.

The next day, my adult children would drive or fly back to their homes, each to grieve in their own way and to live their lives. I felt so alone. It was like I had been airlifted and dropped into a dry and thirsty desert. I needed to figure out how to put one foot in front of the other.

In the days that followed, an endless sea of people stopped by the house, bringing food and well-intended condolences. In passing weeks, our mail box would fill with cards offering kind words in an attempt to comfort our broken and bleeding hearts. With each kind gesture I felt the deep reality bore into my soul: our son was indeed gone; and he was never returning.

AS I LEARNED TO NAVIGATE THIS NEW REALITY, I searched for answers. The surgeon had offered to answer any question the family might have concerning the surgery. I couldn't wait to get some answers to all of the *whys* that continued to build in my head.

I took Brenda with me to take notes. We found our way to the third floor of a large medical building attached to the hospital. The waiting room to his office was empty. He must be in surgery often, I thought. The office staff was friendly. Once we mentioned who we were, we were led down a short hallway to his office and told to make ourselves comfortable. We sat in front of a large wooden desk and immediately noticed that we were staring at a large map of Spain, framed and hanging on his wall. We got up.

Brenda was checking out the degrees and awards that hung on one wall, "He's the real deal, Rose," she said.

"Brenda," I said, "check this out." I pointed to a statue that boasted of completing the Camino de Santiago.

When we sat, it was almost as though our sitting electrically opened the door for him, and the doctor walked in. His stature was small and he wore blue scrubs covered with a white medical coat with his name neatly embroidered in blue. We shook hands as we exchanged introductions.

"We both noticed," I said, "it looks like you hiked the Camino de Santiago."

The doctor's face broke into a small grin. "Yes, I did," he said.

Without any thought I asked, "How did you get that kind of time off?"

He rounded his desk and sat down, "I skipped ahead by driving," he said, and we all smiled, knowing that was a no-no.

Then the energy in the room changed. He slowly turned his head and stared out the window. His eyes brimmed with tears as he told me that he thought of my son every day.

I told him that I thought of Isaac every second of every day. "Thank you for seeing me, doctor," I continued. "I need you to explain to me, in laymen's terms, what happened to my son."

I stretched my arm and placed one hand on the far left of his desk. "Here I was in Burgos, Spain, on the Camino de Santiago," I said, "when I got the call that my son was in surgery with a top surgeon, given a 90 percent survival rate." I stretched my other arm and placed my right hand on the far right of his desk. "Two hours later," I said, "I was here in Madrid Airport. I called home, and he was dead." I gestured between the spaces of the two points, "I need you to explain to me what happened from here, to here."

He replied that he just did not know why the surgery went wrong—that he had done it successfully in the past, many times, and he had only lost one other patient, many years ago. His manner seemed sincere.

He then asked if it would help if I saw pictures of the procedure.

"Absolutely," I said.

He stood and removed a large medical book off the shelf, placing it open-faced before us. It clearly showed what an aortic dissection was, and also the procedure for repair. However, by the time we had finished with our tour of the human heart, its function, malfunction and repair, I still had no clear answers as to why my son died. I understood the procedure, not the outcome.

"Where did it go wrong?" I asked.

The doctors eyes brimmed with tears as he humbly admitted he didn't know. "His heart became floppy," he said.

"Floppy?" I asked. "What do you mean?"

"His heart just would not beat."

The room filled with a cold silence as his words hung in the air. Just the thought of it made me cry.

I dried my tears and then rose and shook his hand. The thought went through my head that this soft, gentle hand had touched my son's heart.

The hospital report I received a few weeks later said the surgeon had compressed my son's heart for twenty minutes, using his hands to try to get the heart to beat. Isaac died at 2:00 a.m. on October 25, 2016.

IN NOVEMBER I ORDERED THE NECKLACE FOR MARY. MY plan was to give it to her on their anniversary on December 3rd. It would have been their twelfth.

When I arrived to pick up the necklace, a tall, well-dressed, soft-spoken woman welcomed me. She was familiar with our funeral, and with Isaac's passing. She handed be a dark blue velvet box.

I slowly opened it. There it was; a beautiful, silver fingerprint necklace. I glanced up at her and we both wept.

She hugged me and whispered, "Now, when are you going to order yours?"

For the first time during this entire ordeal, I felt heard and I felt honored as Isaac's mother. She had validated my brokenness, and my need.

Two months later, when I called to order my own necklace, she said, "I've been waiting for your call."

My necklace arrived in the spring, as the flowers bloomed and new beginnings surrounded me.

Robb Astor

a white stone in my pocket

so i returned
and found great boulders
in the overgrown fields
standing like immense scattered teeth

or doors refusing to open
cold to the touch
i pressed my ear to each one
to the implacable silence
their absence of words

in my hand a once familiar implement
which i could not recall the purpose of
rusted and broken

strangers approached
from a rattle-trap car they'd abandoned
an old couple bearing a basket
of confused and flopping fish

the woman clung to my arm
told me the moon had fallen into the ocean
then they entered the boulder
and a terrible loneliness came over me

i beat on the boulder
said i was a keeper of stones
please open up
it was no use
the fish were dead

then i remembered
what the implement was for
but when i bored a hole in the sky
only hornets spilled out

Amanda Forrester

Red Rose Tea

It is estimated that more than 300 million Wade figurines have been given away in packages of Red Rose Tea in America.
—RedRoseTea.com

I find it packed away
your box of Red Rose Tea
even after all these years
the fragrance is strong and fresh
I tremble as I lift the lid

I close my eyes and remember
the pots of tea we shared
with scoops of sugar and splashes of milk
I see the smile of a little boy
with a china cup too big for his hands
and tea stains on the table cloth
signs of a life being lived

I see the smile of my boy, now a man
with hands too big for the china cup
hands that tremble
from the secrets you try to hide
tea stains on the table cloth
signs of a life in struggle
but I don't know how to help you

My eyes open to the here and now
your box of Red Rose Tea is nearly full
only a few bags used
the ceramic figurine is still there
in the lower right corner
I hold it in my hand

A Peregrine falcon
a raptor, a bird of prey
whose name means "to wander"
fastest flying bird in the world
with hooked beak, strong talons
soaring overhead it dives at two hundred miles per hour
catching its prey in mid-flight
there is no escape

I am gripped by the talons of grief
carried away without warning or rescue
ripped apart by the Peregrine falcon
that I found in your Red Rose Tea.

Angela Haase

Used Car Auction

I swear it was Billy's car in the Bendon Eagle's auction lot.
Not many '68 Chevy Impala ss 427's Butternut Yellow
with Tuxedo Black tops in this corner of the state.
I had to turn back and pull over to check it out.
I peeked inside at the cracked tuck and roll upholstery.
He was always going to order a kit to fix it.
Instead, we threw Mexican blankets over the seats,
unsnapped the top, took off. Sometimes I'd pack a cooler.
Or we'd stop at the Friendly for burgers and beers.
Especially in September--the last hurrah of summer
when you get one cloudless Saturday in the 70's, the reds
early to bleed into the canopy of leaves along the coast
of M-22 to Empire. We'd go further if it stayed warm.
Sometimes he'd head inland, past Schmidt's pig farm.
Their boars would go half a ton before slaughter.
On a good straightaway, Billy 'd open it up to show off.
I'd pull my ponytail tight. He'd throw his head back,
grinning, taking in the sun. The last time I saw Billy
was at his uncle's funeral. He wouldn't look at me.
I didn't sign the guestbook. The last I saw his car
it was in the driveway of a stonecutter's place
whose work was featured in Architectural Digest.

Billy bartered the car for mosaics of fish in his bathroom
and marble counters for the kitchen. If he'd paid cash,
maybe the guy would have made his bills and not put
the gun in his mouth just after his fortieth birthday,
a few months after he opened his showroom. I went to his
grand opening and sat with him. We talked about the holy
coolness of the granite samples. Felt them to our cheeks.
We ate peaches and let the juice run down our wrists.

Anne-Marie Oomen

Promise

There is no bargain with the dead, no arrangement or negotiation, and yet, sometimes I wonder if there isn't some exchange that happens afterwards, if there isn't a process by which the psychic energy is rearranged and, well, promises are made in some realm we don't comprehend. When David's father Bob died shortly before our wedding, I wanted him back in the worst way. I wanted him there for his son, for our ceremony, to witness our joy. I wanted him present. He had died suddenly of a heart attack just five weeks before our wedding day, coming in from walking the dog late one winter evening, announcing that it was so cold it took his breath, and then getting in to his recliner to watch TV, and a few minutes later, just gone. That's how David's stepmom described it. Just gone.

The morning after, David called me here in Northern Michigan just before my school day began, and because it was not unusual for us to chat in the morning, I didn't think anything awry, launched into my news, prattling on about a new poem just published until at last I noticed his quiet, and he told me. Quiet, steady. I was the one who broke.

I hadn't known Bob for long, had spent only half a dozen occasions with him, but I had been impressed. He was like my own beloved dad, quiet and steady, which is where David gets it. He and my dad were both World War II vets. David and I suspect that they were in Italy with the Allies during the same years; they both had that weight of history leaning on them. You can tell with those old vets, their faces. As David and I became more serious, I wanted Bob to like me. I wanted to make him proud that David had chosen me. I wanted Bob to believe that David had chosen well, and that I would make David happy. But I knew enough about marriage—having failed in one—to know that it's all practice and not a little luck.

I do think Bob and I liked each other, but in a rote way—we just didn't have time to go deeper. So I had no way of knowing if he really saw me. But shortly before he died, at my first annual Christmas with the Early clan in their old family home in St. Louis, Kingsbury Place, a moment told me what he was about.

I had chosen carefully what I considered a great evening outfit for their Christmas Eve dinner: a deep teal silk blouse, tightly fitted at the waist, a flowing black silk skirt layered over a ruffled underskirt of fine cotton in that nineties midi length. The ruffled slip was lacey and intended to show, a tease under the black silk. Very stylish at the time. Though now I cringe, I was confident that outfit was a showstopper on that important evening.

Somewhere in the middle of the festivities, Bob had pulled David aside. Shortly after, David came to me, looking uncertain. He nudged me into the stairwell, and said, "My Dad wants you to know your slip is showing. My Dad is worried about your slip." I flushed, pissed and humiliated.

"It's supposed to show." I'm sure I snapped.

David looked pained, "I know." He smiled, "I love it, but he thinks it's showing. He's … worried for you."

It took me a minute. Thoughts raced: he was an older man who didn't know anything about style, he was embarrassed by the idea of a woman's slip showing, and finally: he was protecting me from embarrassment. He was protecting me. He had chosen the most tactful way he could think to protect me and … his son, and it meant he had seen me—though perhaps not the way I had hoped. My irritation faded. I slipped into the bathroom and hiked the underskirt up and tucked it under the belt, and despite the bulge, and my love of lace, I wore the black skirt without any lace showing at all for the rest of the evening, and Bob, bless him, was as warm and kind to me as he had ever been. It seemed like the beginning of something.

Two weeks later he was gone.

After the shock of loss settled, I mostly grieved not knowing him better, and for my beloved David whose father would not see us married. And then of course, the question rose of how his death would affect our plans. Because all that week of the funeral, we considered postponing the wedding. We walked along the Meramac River outside of St. Louis, a long path bordering the flood plain, and talked about waiting. I wanted the right thing for David. That January loss coming so close to our mid-February wedding meant the entire family would still be in grief. What would that do for a day intended to be joyous. The mature woman in me said, let David and his brother get past that. But selfishly, I didn't want to wait. The less mature me was afraid that if we waited, it would never happen. Why did I think that? Was I uncertain? But there on the barren winter path, David turned to me, said sincerely he wanted to go ahead. That sealed it. It would be a smaller, more intimate wedding, but yes, we would proceed as planned.

I was relieved. And I suspect we all wanted something joyous to anticipate.

FIVE WEEKS LATER, THE AFTERNOON AFTER VALENTINE'S Day, we waited for our cues in the Great Hall at the old Armour Mansion in Lake Forest, a place of ostentatious marble and a pastiche of Italian Renaissance formality. We waited in the great hall to enter a side room, an intimate library, just right for us, full of comfortable old furniture and beautiful books. David kept taking deep breaths and then smiling at me, reassuring me or himself, I'm not sure. I kept forgetting things. The day was February cold, Midwest foggy, an all morning drizzle. When the time came, fog rolled in and created, oddly enough, a private cloud around the windows of the library where our families had gathered. We were closed in and it was … fine, a kind of floating island as a wedding day should be, just without the sun. I was dressed in the ivory tea length lace-all-over dress that I loved and that I have to believe Bob would have at last approved, there being no question about a slip. We entered the stunning old library lined with rare hardcovers. The caterers handed us the trays of champagne to pass out so people (we!) would sip (and relax) before our vows.

I'd like to say it was when I handed my own elderly father the champagne that the thought first came to me, but I don't know that for sure. As the forty people gathered in that formal room, as we passed out the delicate flutes, a strange certainty arrived, hard to express in words. Thoughts of Bob had permeated that morning. Our grief was still keen and even after five weeks, sharp as a knife, especially for David. We were glad to be marrying, glad to have gathered closest friends and family, but we missed

Bob, and though we would remember him, we hoped his absence would be compensated with joy. We'd said as much to each other, and held each other in that hope.

But as I passed out that champagne, a sudden clarity in that fog-circled room: *this death has guaranteed your happiness.* Not a voice as much as a conviction: some powerful knowing. How could that be? No one bargains with death, not even the dead. It's not even cool to think that one life was bargained for another. But as I greeted people, the feeling remained: some kind of psychological projection? Some mental quirk of emotion and the need for comfort? But once the thought was there, it persisted. I don't want to mislead: one life had not been traded for another, but rather, here was … an assurance, almost a … promise in the very air, and it wasn't just the one David and I would utter. Our happiness was promised, and it had something to do with Bob's absence.

Standing before palladium windows where the fog pressed hard against the glass, we said our vows. When I had finished mine, a long-winded meandering set of promises about taking long walks and practicing patience, David uttered his one-line vow. A stunningly brief and true vow. His vow, "I promise to make it all easier." I was startled and then I felt it, that deep shift, and knowledge. Yes, a covenant sealed. And I knew then in that aftermath of a father's death, in that other unspoken promise about our lives, that no matter what happened in the material world, our internal happiness was in that moment contained and extended into time.

The promise has not failed us.

Greta Bolger

The things that own us

accumulate as though of their own volition
multiplying exponentially until we have fifty blankets,
one thousand forks. Inconveniently, people keep dying,
leaving their dishes, sheets and new shoes behind.

Young people, scared people, poor people
hold on to everything, broken, dirty, useless
or not. I shed things like snake skin, writhing out
of the memories that permeate

what once belonged to the gone ones—
the dish she made gravy in, his Iron Maiden hoodie.
I used to go to rummage sales, resale stores,
the thrill of the hunt. Now, it's the winnowing

that satisfies, taut black bags full of goods
that can't weigh me down anymore, moved on
to cover the beds and backs of strangers near
and far, like the man I saw sitting on a curb

in Nebaj, Guatemala, who wore a fleece
from the states embroidered with "Coach's Wife,"
warmed on that cool mountain morning
by an anonymous coat, neither knowing nor caring

why the coach was no longer the coach
or the wife was no longer the wife.

Elaine McIntosh

African Sky

Twenty six years after my husband died
I took the money left from some
insurance policy he never bought,
went on Safari in the Okavango Delta
where elephants bathe, pluck plants,
wash them clean of sand
to avoid grinding down their teeth.
Slow, big footed mammals
on the move, in line and alone.

Hundreds of tiny Carmine Bee Eaters,
their brilliant red breasts saturating the sky,
another sunset before settling
in trees like wind-buffeted flowers.

The soft-voiced, graceful Botswana guides driving
    the jeeps
were as fascinated by the old woman traveling alone
as I was by how they got there.
Tracking lions, following herons to the rookery,
we could ask about each other. One asked if
there are Christians in America. I asked
if they are happy.

My favorite guide had two daughters
and a wife studying to be a chef. We
stopped the jeep during a night drive
to watch the stars come out in the clear sky.
He told me his father taught him everything he knew
identifying each bird, plant, animal
from a life lived in the Delta.

His father died when he was sixteen.
Now thirty, he missed him every day.
I shared how my children had become
biologists like their Dad,
trying to find him in a world
left empty by his death.

We watched the Southern Cross
rise in the African sky,
the vast spill of the Milky Way
surrounded by constellations
so different than the ones
I find in my own night sky.

Mary Anna Kruch

What Lingers

As my mother grew older,
she developed a preference for French perfume.
The fragrance followed her
from the bath to her rocking chair
and nestled into the afghan
she threw over her knees.

Before her last surgery,
my mother had set out her will—
noting to whom her emerald ring should go,
the contents of the safety deposit box,
and her wish for a simple memorial.
Still, no one ever tells you
about having to take back the gifts you gave,
photographs you framed,
birthday cards you sent,
afghan you crocheted.

When my brothers and I entered the house,
It was as though she never left—
here a Sinatra record out of its sleeve,
there an Agatha Christie book open,
peppermint gum tucked into a drawer;
an oil painting
of her father's barn
sat unfinished at an easel.

In her closet, blouses and slacks
were deftly arranged by color;
a painting by her sister Marian
leaned against the back wall—
Mom drowsing on an arm chair,
sixteen and apple cheeks aglow.
A leather folder on the shelf above
held Dad's first paycheck stub,
a copy of their marriage license,
Mom's army discharge papers,
and the love letters—

I reimagine her in White Horse, Alaska;
winter is lit by young lovers' kisses
against the white-puffed air.
Loose, yellowed photographs
tucked into thin paper slide out,
reveal love wrapped in coats and scarves—
unmistakable heat.

We sell the house,
disperse furniture,
divide checks among siblings.
But no one tells you about
the random dial of numbers—
numbers found by fingers
as easily

as in years past.
The ring is hollow,
empty, unanswered.
A deep longing grows.

But sometimes the creak of her rocking chair
slips into dreams.
Then mornings find my cat fast asleep,
curled into the afghan,
lightly scented with French perfume.

Diana Stover

Color

I wake knowing I am on duty. I make coffee, feed the dog, toast a bagel for Jake and shoo him off to school. I scrutinize the hallway from the living room to the bathroom to assure no rugs or power cords can trip Paul. Walking from room to room, I gather dirty clothes and toss them in the washer.

Paul is awake and is eager to have a clean body, so I help him undress while leaving the brace on his neck. Doctors gave stern warnings to "never take this off" and we comply out of fear. I maneuver his feet over the bathtub edge and, holding his hands, I expect to see him towering over me. Instead, I can see his eyes are parallel with mine. I can't help thinking about *my mountain man* and his robust and viral body. When we met, people told me he resembled Burt Reynolds, and this morning, I see my man with greying hairs that are letting go of their roots. We have known each other's bodies intimately, yet today, I hate seeing my frail husband naked, and cloak my tears.

Once he's clean, I hand him the towel, and then I gently pull a terry cloth strip under the neck brace to make certain it is dry. He tells me, "This feels as good as sex." I obsess on warnings doctors have given about paralysis if any movement jostles the vertebrae in his spine, so I gingerly move the brace so he can shave.

I wrestle clean sheets onto the hospital bed as he settles into his floral recliner. I remind him a friend is coming to be with him while I place snacks and fresh water on the side table. Casper, our cocker spaniel, curls at his feet.

Once assured he is set, I go to work. I mindlessly grip the steering wheel as I locate the homes of the patients I need to visit. Before the day is over, I see seven dying patients. I listen to each of them talk about how they and their loved ones are coping with death. I hold their hands and offer prayers or blessings. After each visit, I pull over on a side street and write up spiritual care plans.

In the quiet of the car, I want someone to write an assessment on me.

I drink a cup of coffee after I get home and am revived to do my evening tasks. Dinner simmers on the stove, while my hands work their way through a dozen childproof caps. I scan the medical bills piling up on the kitchen table in our great room where they are never out of sight. I left paperwork to confirm Paul's permanent disability sticking out of my purse to remind myself it needs a signature.

I see our family living with cancer between us, and I want to deny the idea of Paul's possible death. I have re-arranged our house to let this unwelcome parasite take up residence. A section of the kitchen counter-top is now a designated medicine depository. The bathroom has a high-rise toilet seat, a host of unfamiliar "medically-necessary items" and disinfectants. I repeat to my family and any visitor my new word, "neutropenic." I tell them it means we must wash our hands over and over because a microscopic germ could cause a deadly infection.

The couch—my new bed—is parallel to his hospital bed so I can be certain he lives through the night. He tells me he fights to stay awake till midnight each day, "to say I have lived another day." I am aware that much of his day is filled with prayers and his visions of God's hand resting on each broken space.

Paul insisted that Jake have a *normal* routine for his final years of high school, so our son and I turned the back two rooms of the small house into his bedroom and a gaming area for his friends. I am comforted by the voices of adolescents echoing through the house. Jake's friends are not intimidated by cancer.

I review the names on a list of friends and police officers who volunteered to help us and make calls to prepare a schedule. Our sisters and mothers had been present in the early weeks but had to return to Ohio, Colorado, New Mexico, and Oklahoma. I take a minute to thank God for the blessings of friendship and family.

I hug Jake on his food runs between the kitchen and his hovel. He is present and not present at the same time. I wonder if this is what *normal* looks like for a boy living in this house. I worry about him, as he seems too eager to return to the world of "Final Fantasy."

I yearn to slip into a fantasy world myself. Instead, I steal a couple minutes to take Casper for a walk. My thoughts follow me in to the cold air which jogs my memory of the early spring morning that upended our lives...

PAUL'S VOICE WHISPERED IN MY EAR, "HELP ME."

It was 12:30. I was befuddled by the brain fog of sleep but quickly responded when I heard his sobs and the words, "I can't lift my head. Oh my God, it hurts!"

Jake was spending the night at a friend's house so I couldn't call him to help me get his dad to the hospital. I quickly dressed and pulled sweats over Paul's boxers. He held his hands around his neck as we got his legs to the floor and struggled to the car. The hospital was only three minutes away. I asked the guard to watch Paul's neck as he helped him into a wheel chair and took him through the revolving doors.

After parking the car, I found Paul in a cubicle; his clothes had been replaced with a gown. He was delusional, so I reported on the "flu" I thought Paul had, and told the doctor that Paul had scheduled an x-ray later that week for pains in his back and neck. I added that he had been under a lot of stress the past six months and had lost over 50 pounds.

I didn't tell him that I made Paul, who is usually a stickler for cleanliness, take a bath that morning because he smelled of death.

I waited until sunrise before I ran home to care for the dog and to shower. On the way out the door, I grabbed a Bible and paper to work on a sermon I needed to write for Palm Sunday. I occasionally accepted preaching assignments but work on my manuscripts needed to fit around my fulltime work as a hospice chaplain.

I slipped back into Paul's room and saw he was deep in sleep. I pulled a chair next to the bed and started scribbling notes on the events of the crucifixion, when Jesus says, "Father forgive them, for they know not what they do."

A curtain separated his room from the nurse's station. I overheard someone say, "fractured c-2 vertebrae" and thought, "How tragic is that?"

Several minutes later, a new doctor entered the room.

"We have the results," he said. "Your husband's c-2 vertebra has been blown out by a tumor the size of a small egg. The bones in that area are jagged." He placed a copy of the CT scan on a screen and showed me the spiked teeth of the explosion site. "He has multiple fractures and holes throughout his spine. We see spots that look like someone spooned out pieces of bones from his head to his legs. His kidneys are failing because the calcium from the bones are damaging them. He has cancer, but we need to do more investigating to determine if it is one of four possible cancers." He named them. My brain told my ears to stop listening.

My mouth had gone bone dry. The nurse brought Vaseline and I coated my lips, and I wished I could also coat the inside of my mouth. I couldn't even talk, and my breath kept running away.

It was Sunday morning. Nearly everyone we knew was in church. I didn't know who to call, then I thought of Mary because Jake was at her house. I asked her to have him come to the hospital when he woke up. Within the hour, Mary and Bob walked down the hall bringing a hot cup of coffee.

Jake came with his friends and he held me. I repeated the doctor's descriptions and told him the cancer had a name, Multiple Myeloma. I didn't tell Jake that Paul was in the final stage of the disease. He stood frozen with his 17-year-old sentinels at his side. All I wanted in that moment was for all of this to go away.

I spent every day of that first week beside Paul. The oncologist was maneuvering the system to coordinate a plan to treat an "incurable cancer." He explained that cancer is now *managed*. Nurses were preparing me for his death.

The incongruity in their messages bounced about my head.

The second week I angrily returned to work. My boss informed me that I had no other option: I must fill my role in the hospital; patients needed me. She was wise, but I didn't like it.

I was bolstered by the men and women in police uniforms who came to talk with Paul. He was their chaplain, and they came to return the comfort he had given. Friends, ministers and hospice co-workers brought words of comfort along with food and flowers. Paul's mom came. My neighborhood girlfriends, the "Alleluia Girls," held vigil with me. Seventy-five people visited us.

I became the guardian who wanted to shield Paul, as some people came seeking to confess their part in a church battle that had ended with his resignation three months before. I was still raw from the summer evening when I answered the phone and Paul's wails kept me from recognizing his voice. People had taken sides over a staffing issue. In his room, some of these same people stood over his bed and sought atonement, but Paul was tranquilized. Their words just filled the air. I was not ready to offer forgiveness on his behalf, or on my own.

Daily I walked through the halls from the cafeteria to Paul's room and pondered how the church was a great love of my life—and had so disappointed me. I had naively believed people would never trust lies. I was still bewildered that my friend, one of the Alleluia Girls and the church secretary, had hacked into Paul's email account after we left the church, sharing three ambiguous emails from women to create a narrative about Paul that made me doubt his love for me. I couldn't stop imagining the hallways of the church and the people talking about him.

In the middle of this chaos, I couldn't stop blaming the church for Paul's cancer. I quizzed the doctor about what part stress may have played in exacerbating the spread of the disease. He told me that the cells were "probably in his body for two years and were silently spreading, but an event led them to explode in his body." He confirmed that stress was most likely the trigger.

Daily, I begged God to let Paul live. I prayed that God would help us find healing from this spiritual pain before he died.

At night, as ambient light covered us, I laid my head on the bed and held Paul's hand. Our weekends free after Paul's resignation, we had gone to a bed and breakfast and realized we hadn't had a *date* in eleven years. Paul had apologized to the church for the email conversations, and now we confessed our failures to each other by writing them on slips of paper, then burning them in a glass jar. New promises had been made. I was excited to have new dreams without the demands of the church between us.

Each night I wondered what this cancer would steal from us.

I ruminated on how I missed seeing the signs of his disease. I was a medical professional, trained to look for warnings of diminishing health, yet I failed to see these in my husband. I had attributed his rapid weight loss to stress. I thought I had noticed his diminishing height, but it *had* to be nonsense, so I dismissed it. I had never considered his strong body could be damaged. In my mind, he had been invincible because he never got sick.

The oncologist came to the room once more before Paul was discharged. I was overwhelmed when he said, "If he gets through four or five rounds of chemotherapy, he will need a stem-cell transplant." I asked about the broken bones. He responded, "Nothing can be done. They're too fragile for a surgeon to touch. They will need to heal on their own. Just be very careful. His body is like that of a china doll."

I took Paul home, but he was not the Paul I had been married to for 21 years. This Paul had lost 70 pounds, could not walk, was incontinent and wigged-out on steroids. His neck had an odd crook and he had lost four inches of height. He had a plastic neck collar on and we had been told he could be a quadriplegic with a car accident, or even a slight fall.

MY SOUL HURTS WHILE I WRAP UP MY DUTIES OF THIS day. Inside, I am a crumbled mess, and that mess exhausts me.

Prayer has become my screaming at God or my repeating one scripture from the Bible, "He restores my soul." I read the Psalms over and over, finding affinity with the martyred writer but little comfort. Friends listen but I can't repeat my story *ad nauseum* because it fatigues me even more than them, and I can see their discomfort with my angst. Guided imagery demands my letting go, but I am not ready to let go. The counselor I see is helping but I need the energizing power of the pain right now.

The words "art therapy" come to my mind. I offer it to children who are losing a parent at our hospice. I've made referrals for it to others dealing with unresolved pain. I wonder if it could help me tonight.

I retreat to the back bedroom which is now Jake's game room. I open the closet which is crammed with fabric, threads, yarn and Sunday School junk to make into children's crafts and a million other trinkets. It needs to be decluttered as much as my soul needs clearing.

I find dried-up paint but no paper. I ask Jake to watch his dad while I run to JoAnn's Fabrics.

Again, I rearrange the living room. This time, I shove the couch about a foot across the carpet and place a lamp next to my favorite cushion. The living room portion of the great room is cramped with the love seat, couch, bed, recliner and end tables that are now holding water glasses, tissues, pill cups, and the terry cloth strip used in the evenings to ease the itch under Paul's brace. I look around and recall that I redecorated this room only six months ago. I think, *At least the walls are pretty.*

I find a container and place my paints and a cup of water into it. I pull a tray on to my lap and I reach up to adjust the lampshade. Light illuminates the blank page.

For a moment, I consider that I am not a painter. My mother painted, so I recall how she started her pieces.

I flood the paper with water. Then I pick the color black. I draw a church. I scrawl scraggly, emotion-filled words around the building. I pick harsh colors to illustrate the stained-glass windows. The words are coming from the mouths of those who gossip. The gossiping stick figures only get the most displeasing colors from my pallet.

I place this picture on a towel to dry. On a new page, I lay down red flames that resemble an image of Hell. I draw vengeful demons chasing after designated personalities who have real names. I am disturbed by this painting.

I rise then, and place the two paintings in the laundry room and close the door. I dump the water and put the paint away.

I wonder if this "art therapy" is really such a good idea.

I turn to sleep. All night, the darkness haunts my dreams. Before the sun rises, I feel convicted by the ugliness in these works of art.

The pictures are dry now, and I pick them up. I hate them. I hate me for being someone I don't recognize being mirrored to me in their colors. I rip them to shreds and bury them in the trash bucket outside of the house.

THE NEXT NIGHT, AFTER BEING HAUNTED BY WHAT THE paintings revealed about me, I am eager to create. I have confessed my darkness. I want to see what emerges, as I have set one rule: no ugly.

I select paints named Cerulean blue, ultramarine, violet, yellow, orange, burnt sienna and rose, and fill the holes in my palette. Swathes of color come from the paint brushes at the end of my hands to fill the page. I create sky with various hues diluted with water and allowed to dry. I imagine my mountains and draw them with blues, blacks, browns, purples and white. I layer a variety of greens to make trees enhanced with sienna. I tuck a lake in the foreground. This is my common doodle to bring me back to my innocent beginnings of life in Colorado.

I take another sheet and make a flower. Pink, yellow, brown, plum merge to my liking. Each stroke gives birth to a pansy, a first flower of spring that can endure the harsh frosty nights.

After creating six pages of art, I empty the water and curl up on the couch. I close my eyes. Behind my eyelids, I see color. The words on the tubes of paint fill my thoughts. Pink and blue swishes follow me into my sleep.

I play with techniques and colors. I copy images of dahlias, irises, mums, geraniums, cosmos, and roses from a seed catalog to create a fantasy garden. While painting, I imagine those same flowers going into my yard this spring.

I venture to try images beyond my skill. I am surprised that I can paint a barn. It is old, rustic and starting to fall apart. I use a variety of sienna paints mixed with brown and whites. One day a whimsical dragonfly flitters onto my page. I make her with happy pinks, purples, and teal. I struggle with drawing people, so when a ballerina with disproportionate hands comes to life, I am not surprised at my need to improve the proportion of images that appear in my work.

The best memories of our younger family come to life with pictures of Lake Michigan beaches where we tossed Jake's small body into the air without a care in the world. I paint the dunes, grasses against the various hues of vast blue lake. I feel happy. Many likenesses of Colorado mountains are placed on paper, and I claim the stature of the mountains. I acknowledge my strength.

Each night I compose until six to eight pictures dry on the kitchen table. I stack them next to the medical bills.

All summer, Paul fights the side effects of the chemotherapy, making personal goals to build his body. Jake spends warm days caring for his dad while his friends still fill the backrooms with their laughter, video game sounds, and splashes in the backyard swimming pool. I work holding the hands of the dying and find hope in their stories, while I reconcile with my own.

I rediscover my voice with God. I forgive myself through the releasing of the ugly. Counseling helps me figure out how to live without a vengeful justice. Friends and family stay steady, and I let go of those who have betrayed me.

§   §   §

WE WERE FORTUNATE THAT CANCER RESEARCH PARAL-leled Paul's diagnosis, and Paul lived a functional and fun life for eleven more years. He was able to see Jake graduate from college and find Evan, the love of his life.

Paul died on our 33rd anniversary, after calling me to his bedside to give me two beautiful kisses while Jake and Evan held his hands. I believe his peaceful death beautifully completed our love story.

Painting became the silent space in the middle of our busy. I used color to create beauty and it altered my thinking. Painting calmed my soul and let me conclude each day through a season I never fully understood. Peace came. My most sincere prayer was answered.

Kirk S. Westphal

Putting Away Plates

Time spent in spindrift
Time you don't get back.
The meal has long been over
and forgotten,
spontaneous communion,
formality of prayer and bread
broken into genuine disinterest
of the day.
Salted pork in Worcestershire
and apples baked to stew
helping water now
resist the drain,
That's all.
Don't give up the day.
But dishes, warm and damp
because the towel's never dry,
Uplifted to the cupboards
in hands newly softened and slowed—
Flowers at the headstone
In memoriam.

Roo Davison

White with Orange Lettering

I stepped up to the edge
looked down
saw your head
wrapped in a plastic bag
white with orange lettering
Sainsburys—where good food costs less

I didn't know then
that it was my head in there

I touch your chest
stone cold
The man on the phone
orders me to take off the bag
But I can't bear
coming face to face with you

On the floor by your chair
tape, bits of string.
I pick up a pair of scissors
cut a small hole in the bag
just below your nose
just in case you're still breathing

I'm sorry
I know it's too late
I know it's only a gesture
It's the best I can do

It's mostly a blur now
screaming and crying and
police and ambulances and
questions and wailing and
waiting and wishing and baby
sisters who don't understand

As if anyone understands

Only odd details remain, stuck
the chipped yellow Formica
of the kitchen table
we crawled over when we broke in
A cup and saucer in the sink
The half-eaten packet of digestive biscuits
red wrapper neatly folded down
to keep them fresh

Three weeks later I'm swimming
don't ask me why
a swimming pool
of all places
I suddenly wake up
realize I've been asleep
all that time
dreaming the same dream
over and over

Stepping up to the edge
looking down
seeing your face, my face
wrapped in a plastic bag
white with orange lettering

Greta Bolger

Women Friends

The mystery of those ties
how they hold you up when a child dies
or a spouse wanders, how they turn
a kitchen full of steam and tomato guts
into a day of pure joy, help you pick out
glasses, pick strawberries, pick up
your black dress for your mother's funeral,
help you zip yourself into that dark day.

Once, in the woods of Minnesota
we gathered with our teacher, a deceived wife
of a famous poet, to tell what little we knew
about how women intricately knot themselves together
with secrets and sharing hours and lives
and then, as abruptly as if burned or cut apart,
fall away into dangling unravelment.

Three well-loved women went, to paraphrase.
One because a domineering husband
didn't like how little I liked him. One
because she doesn't want me to watch
her fail and die. The last over a party invitation
that was not mine to make.
Years of heart work, like a ruby on a gold chain
dropped willfully down the sewer grate.

Susan Odgers

Hope Changes

R ecently at a party, I met a man in his late 70s who told
me his adult daughter was undergoing treatment for
advanced stage brain cancer. As the patriarch of the family,
he said, he was holding all of them together.

He also said he was holding his daughter's hope.

She'd grown weary of all of the various treatments and
was very depressed. Even her own daughters didn't seem
to hold her focus. Her dad sighed. "I'm exhausted from
trying to be so positive. I'm constantly fighting against
the hopelessness."

When I asked him what kept him going, he started to
cry. "No one ever asks me that," he said.

At the same party, I also met a young couple. They
are parents of an infant, so this was a rare night out for
them. After we chatted about one thing or another, they
told me their son, their first child, had cystic fibrosis. I
listened as they shared how much they loved him. The
mom said his symptoms were minimal. I asked where he'd
been getting his medical care. Downstate, they said, at a
children's hospital.

The dad said, "I doubt we're ever going back there."

Before I could say anything, he added, "We've found
the care abusive. Not helpful. The whole approach seems

to be based upon hopelessness. They offer few positive actions we can take. We can't parent that way. They seem to want to take away our hope. We're going to let our son show us what he needs. We'll find another facility."

The next day, I saw my mother-in-law, Margaret, who is 90 years old. She was married to the same man for more than 65 years until his death. She's a mother, grandmother and great-grandmother. She's recently been through some health challenges and change in her living environment.

I asked her about hope as an elderly person.

"Hope never ends," she said. "It's not just for younger people. Many people may think that my life is over—I've lived my best days. But each day, I get out of bed with a sense of hope. I want to see what happens next in my life. I especially want to see how my loved ones' lives unfold. I'm interested in what happens in the world. At 90, I have healed, tried again, gotten better and regained some of my independence. I've seen doctors lose hope in what they can do for their patients. Often, the patient then loses hope. I've also experienced really hopeful care. Equally, false hope isn't helpful. It's not hope."

More than 35 years ago, after training in a doctoral program at Wayne State University, I became a mental health therapist. I was in my late 20s. Years earlier, when I was eighteen, I'd had a spinal stroke, rendering me a paraplegic.

The first time I opened the door to my office, I worried that my wheelchair would frighten people away; instead, it brought them to me. "You've had to create a life for yourself in the midst of great loss," they said. "You couldn't change what happened to you. Just like us. You're exactly the person we want to be working with."

I've often held others' hope when they've felt or thought they were hopeless. I've seen people use hope as a placebo and get better. I've watched people struggle with fear, ego and panic—terrified that to hope meant vulnerability and defeat. Every family of origin has beliefs about hope and how it can and cannot help people. The sources of hope can vary: other people, themselves, nature, faith, education, politics, the arts and science.

In many ways, the best part of hope is that it can energize. Solutions can be found with hope. Hope battles passivity; it empowers and inspires. Hope laughs and lets you know you're not alone. With hope, you believe and trust that you can overcome the insurmountable. You see others do it. Change is possible. You're motivated. Hope allows a person to live their values, no matter what, with greater dignity.

I've known many people without hope. I've seen the places where they live and what hopelessness does to everyone around them. I've seen how hopelessness can suck the very life out of a room.

I've also seen people waste away their lives, wishing, waiting, living "if only." People fall to the seduction that any dream is possible, every ending a fairy tale. Some people hope for the wrong things. They have too much desire, expecting wishes to be fulfilled without effort or desperately trying to control the seeming randomness of life.

Early in my disability, one of my kid sisters asked me what I'd wish for if I were ever on the TV show *Fantasy Island*.

I said I'd like to become a journalist.

She looked at me in horror. "Why didn't you say you wanted to walk again?"

She had a point. Yet I knew the spontaneous answer I had given was the truth: "I now know that I'm going to be okay not walking. I want other things."

In that instance, I also realized that there was more than a wheelchair in place of what was gone. I'd lost my illusion that I could control every aspect of my life. Gone was the "fear of worst things happening." I learned that I wasn't one thing: a walker. What mattered was not just what was gone, but what was strong. One of the best, most helpful compliments my father paid me during my rehabilitation was, "You're going to be okay. You have a good mind."

Quietly, I made several promises to myself: no comparing now to my "before" life, no asking *why me?* but instead *why not me?* and to emphasize my daily progress over perfection.

I also remember not continuously praying that I would walk again. Many people told me to pray for this, but it never really seemed right to me. Instead, I hoped that my paralysis wouldn't break my heart. Even at the age of eighteen, I knew that if my heart closed, I would live a very small life. With an open heart, perhaps more than I imagined could happen.

I've now used a wheelchair for over sixty percent of my life. I was right.

Nora Liu Robinson

The Move

I take one last look around the room. Only the cream-colored floors and cinder block walls appear the same as before. Although it has never felt homey, the room looks strangely empty now without the picture frames and stacks of greeting cards from the past three months. I pick up a vase of flowers from last week's birthday party, cross to the bathroom in three swift steps, pour the water into the sink, then tilt the flowers into the tiny trash can. One surprisingly green stem still bears a tag that reads, "Happy 67th Birthday, Sherm!" He has always been so proud of his birthdate that I used to dread when someone like a receptionist would ask for it.

"My birthdate is a poker straight," my father would announce, triumphantly drumming the counter with his fingers. I would look from my father's expectant grin to the receptionist's polite confusion.

"He means his birthdate is January 23rd, 1945," I'd explain, trying to let my voice communicate embarrassment and solidarity. "That's one, two-three, four-five."

I step out of the bathroom and return the vase to the nightstand. I'm wearing my coat, and I already feel uncomfortably warm. From the bed, I grab the heart-shaped pillow that was my father's "gift" from the American Cancer

Society when he left the hospital in Grand Rapids and moved into this place. The pillow is a floral, baby blue flannel and obviously handmade. I shove it into a nearby plastic bag full of hangers, pick up the bag, and leave the room.

They are waiting at the nurses' station for me. With their backs against the wall are my dad's childhood friend Corky and his wife. They have just retired to their cottage, and they have offered to come today to help with the move. Across from them is my mother, whom my father has recently divorced. When I collected her from the airport, I noticed the wrinkles around her eyes. Today, those worry lines are prominent as she grips the handles of my father's wheelchair.

My father sits slumped, staring at his own lap. He has been diagnosed with glioblastoma, a rare and aggressive brain cancer. Because of the location of the tumor in my father's brain, he can hardly move or even speak. He has been in that bent-over position for weeks, and he hasn't spoken above a whisper in months—not since the day in early October when he was diagnosed. On that day, my brother and I had asked him if he wanted our mom to fly back to Michigan from Colorado, where she had been living with our sister after our parents' separation. My dad said no—twice. We tried to explain his wishes to my mom, but she came back, anyway. She has basically spent every waking moment by his side since then. Today, my mom has him dressed in a navy blue winter coat and a thick beanie I've never seen before. I wonder if she dug through the old closets and basement boxes when she moved back into "his" house. My father is wearing his signature maize-and-blue University of Michigan slippers.

As I approach, my mom, Corky, and his wife turn to

look at me. The hangers bang my leg as I walk. Somewhere down the hall, an alarm goes off—a low-pitched beep that means someone wants to go to the bathroom or has become unclipped from a bed. I walk through the human aisle they have made: past my dad and mom, past Corky and his wife, to the nurse shuffling papers at the desk. "We're all ready to go, I think."

The busy nurse peers over the counter at my dad in the wheelchair and her expression softens. "We sure are going to miss you, Sherman!" Then she turns back to me and says, "Okay, I'll just make a quick copy of his discharge papers. I'll be right back."

A man in his fifties, passing by, asks, "Getting out of here?" He leans on a crutch and has a brace on one knee.

I glance from the man to the front doors and the shuttle idling outside. I look back at the man. He has stubble on his face and a baseball cap that says "Miller Lite."

"Yep," I say, hoping I sound hopeful. "We're heading out." I shift the bag of hangers to my other hand.

The friendly man rests an arm on the support rail attached to the wall and nods approvingly at my father. "That's great, man. Congratulations!" He nods a little while longer, then turns and limps down the hall.

"Ma'am?" The nurse has already returned. She holds an envelope toward me. A logo in the upper left-hand corner reads "Tendercare-Birchwood Health Center" above a green ink image of a birch tree, the name "Sherman Robinson" handwritten in the center. I take the envelope and shove it into the bag of hangers. "Have you already talked to Sandy about paying the rest of your bill?"

"Oh," I say. Sandy. Ugh. It feels like every time I set foot in this place, Sandy pounces on me as though she has been lying in wait all day; insurance has declined this or my dad owes that. One thing I definitely will not miss is Sandy's head popping around every corner. "I thought insurance was covering him through today."

My mother looks at me with alarm. "Nora, we don't need to pay, right?"

"I don't know, Mom." Today, of all days, I need to keep my patience. "I just said, I thought we didn't need to. I called the insurance last week." We both look expectantly at the nurse.

She shrugs apologetically and says, "You'll have to talk to Sandy. She's not in today."

"Okay," I say, relieved. "I'll try to touch base with her."

My mom cuts in, "Now, I have a question."

I look at the nurse and think, *Here we go.* My mom is Chinese, and in her thirties she moved to the U.S. as a refugee from Vietnam. The day she moved to the U.S. was the very first day she thought about the English language or American culture. Her English has come a long way, but talking to "official" people like medical staff isn't her strength. My dad was always the one who handled bills, researched options, read the fine print, and made important decisions, but my mom has never let her linguistic challenges prevent her from voicing her concerns—and she tends to have a lot of concerns. After the divorce, it was my sister who helped her. Now, it's my turn.

With the nurse's attention on her, my mom forges on. "Can you order a van for today? I think it's little too hard to do by ourself now." My mom lets go of the wheelchair and leans confidentially toward the nurse. "You know, Nora not too strong enough to move Sherm in her car anymore. Not too good."

"Mom." I can hear exasperation creeping into the edges of my voice. "I already ordered it. Look." I gesture with the hangers toward the door.

I glance at my father, who must surely be sweating now. I try to sound sunny as I ask, "Well, Dad, are you ready to go?" My mother leaves the counter and resumes her position behind his wheelchair.

My father lifts his eyes off his lap, up to meet mine. This simple gesture strains him. I see the veins in his neck bulge in the effort to raise his head. His mouth opens and his shoulders drop a little as he forces out air. He is trying to talk.

"What?" I set the hangers down and take a step closer, bending myself almost horizontal to put my ear directly in front of his mouth. "I'm sorry, I didn't hear that," I say, a little too loudly. "Can you say it again?"

My father speaks again, and this time I feel the dry air on my ear, I smell the sweetness of his breath. In the beginning, I thought my mom was sneaking him ice cream and chocolate at night—a woman's last-ditch effort to comfort a dying man. I can still remember the day the oncologist opened my father's mouth with a tongue depressor, revealing a field of creamy white bumps dotting the top of his tongue.

"Thrush," the oncologist had declared in the tense stillness of his office. "That's what smells so sweet. It's a fungus, a side effect of chemo."

With my ear this close to my father's mouth, I can almost feel the sticky sweetness of the thrush. His whisper is quiet and strained, but for the first time in two weeks I can make out what he says: the one small word I have been dreading.

"Where?"

I straighten up a little so I can see my father more clearly. "You're moving to a nicer place. It's called Munson Hospice House. We talked about this, remember?" Only it's all wrong because we didn't talk about this and I know it. I had talked with the oncologist and the neurologist and Birchwood's doctor and my mom and Corky—all in my dad's presence—but I had been careful never to say the word "hospice" in front of him.

My father shakes his head. It's nearly imperceptible.

"No, really, you'll like it there. The atmosphere is much better."

My father shakes his head again.

I look at Corky and his wife. They have just driven the better part of an hour for this move. I have already had a private meeting with the Hospice House, I have already completed all the necessary paperwork, I have taken yet another day off work, and they are waiting for us now. Sandy calls me every day about the thousands of dollars we already owe for my dad's daily lodging and care here at Birchwood, and his insurance won't cover any more days. He will need to move into a shared room in the long-term care section at the back of the nursing home, not the large, single-person rooms at the front of the facility reserved for patients undergoing short-term rehabilitation. Insurance only covers short-term rehab if there's an "indication of improvement," and my father hasn't shown any for a week now. And we all know he won't.

I look at my dad. "Would you rather stay here? We can move your stuff back in." I glance at the nurse, who seems preoccupied. Is she listening? I wonder how often this happens.

My mom says, "Nora, we already moved everything. Now what?"

"He doesn't know what he's saying," Corky offers helpfully.

I don't know what to do, but everyone is looking at me. "Okay, then." I straighten up, lift the bag of hangers off the floor, and say, "Let's go." I step back to clear a path for my mom and the wheelchair, and she starts to push.

Immediately my father's eyes grow wide and wild, his milk chocolate irises darting everywhere. My mom takes another step, and with a sudden force of energy, my father kicks his feet, heels-first, off the metal footrests of the wheelchair. His Michigan slippers slam to the shiny, tiled floor, and he splays out into a full-body brake. He looks heroic: Superman flying in front of the derailing train, digging long deep trails into the earth to stop it just before it drops off the cliff. My mother tries to move forward again, but my father's hands fly to the armrests for leverage. He forces his entire body so taut that he trembles.

This is the most impressive display of strength I have seen from my father in the three months since his diagnosis, and I know I will never see such fire again.

In my mind's eye, we stay frozen like this: me with that flimsy bag of hangers and that baby blue pillow poking out, my mom's pained expression, Corky and his wife looking on, my father with shaking hands clutching the metal arms of a borrowed wheelchair, eyes wild and legs splayed, U of M slippers up like a shield against the doors and the world.

Later, I will play and replay my options. I could have gone out and told the driver not to wait for us anymore, and I could have told the nurse that we would just take a double room in the long-term care wing. For that matter,

I could have moved my father back to short-term care and paid out-of-pocket until my father's savings were entirely spent, and then I could have spent my own. I could have invited everyone into the overly floral, mauve-and-hunter-green lounge to talk things over one more time, and in that meeting I could have told my mom and Corky that there's no rush—no rush at all. That if we get to decide one thing in this life, it should be how we exit.

I could do any of those things, but I don't.

Instead, all I do is hold that bag of hangers and watch my father, transfixed. Then after several moments, my father's arms and legs slacken, and his head drops back down. His toes fall so that his slippered feet rest gently on the floor, and my mom can push the wheelchair again. I lead us slowly toward the front doors of the nursing home, toward the shuttle, and toward the sparse, swirling flakes of the late January snow waiting beyond.

Elaine McIntosh

From Darkness

My daughter's pregnant belly,
swollen like two halves
of a beaver dam over her river body,
struggles to carry her twin boys
through the winter
in their separate placental dens.
These boys have tried to
break free too soon. She steadfastly
refuses to let go, despite the dangers
to her own body. She focuses
daily on their belligerency,
quieting to bed rest,
warming her belly with her hands,
stroking the elbows and knees
that will swim to the surface.
I tuck the quilt tightly over them,
swaddling them all
as her father and I did
when she was a newborn.

These boys will cross
from their darkness to our light
on the anniversary of her father's death.
When they arrive, I warm them
against my chest
feeling the beat
of their grandfather's heart.

Greta Bolger

Our Dead Come Home for Christmas

What a surprise, the bony knock at the door just as
we were sitting down to dinner, and then there they all
were, wearing red sweaters, plaid pants, feathered hats
and rhinestone brooches, witty costumes that, like them,
had seen better days. Think Goodwill for ghouls. Sure,
it was great to see them, their giant smiles and big eyes,
though it was hard to tell them apart at first, but once
they started talking, we knew who was who: Daddy
Ralph and Roberta, Grandma T and Harry, Momma
Sue and Red, young George and baby Ben. What a
surprise, like I said, and Bob got out the video camera
and interviewed them about the afterlife while the food
got cold, and then we went into the living room to open
presents and of course we didn't have anything to give
them because who knew? I tried to ignore the bone dust
on the furniture and the incessant grinning, but I have
to admit, I was glad when their time ran out and they
trundled back down the front walk and back to wherev-
er they came from. I know I sound selfish, but sheesh.
That's not what Christmas is all about, is it? And the
videos were completely blank, not a trace they were ever
here in the first place. The minute they left, I poured a
double bourbon and lit myself a cigarette, my first one in
eight and a half years.

Penny Parkin

Heroes

T he winter of 2013 was brutally cold, with record amounts of snow and ice. I contacted Spencer's friends about meeting up at the Guggenheim. We spent a frozen Sunday afternoon in January there, their striped leggings, chunky boots and pom-pom hats contrasting with the stark black-and-white minimalist paintings on the curved white walls of the museum. Afterwards, we ate vegan Chinese food. I felt supremely grateful that they would travel from the far edges of Brooklyn to spend the day with me.

On the train home, I couldn't help but overhear the woman sitting next to me conversing with her husband across the aisle. They were discussing an academic paper they were both reading, chock-full of complex mathematical equations. I guessed they were professors, as this train would be stopping in Princeton.

She probably noticed I was looking at her paper and after a few minutes she turned to me. "I'm trying to read this, but I just can't get into it."

"It looks pretty challenging," I began. "I could never—"

"Yeah, well, it's written by a woman I've worked with and I have to read it for a conference I'm going to in Vienna in a few weeks."

"Oh, nice! My daughter was supposed to go to a

conference there, but she had to cancel it because she had another conference in California right afterwards and she thought the jet lag would do her in. So, do you teach at Princeton?"

"No, I'm on the faculty at the University of British Columbia, but I'm on sabbatical at the Institute for Advanced Studies in Princeton."

"I've never been to British Columbia, but I hear it's gorgeous," I responded.

"It is. But I have a beautiful office at the Institute and I can look out over the grounds—it's like sixty acres. Just beautiful."

"Hmm, yeah. I guess that's why it's called the 'ivory tower,' right?" I tried for a bit of humor.

"Well, it's also wonderful because my son is at Princeton and I get to see him a lot, which has been great. My husband's also on sabbatical, so it's just worked out really well. My daughter is back in Vancouver, but we're really close and we Skype each other every day."

"Lucky you. I only talk with my daughter every two weeks or so. She teaches European History at Colby. It's her first full-time position. She was at Georgetown last year, doing a post-doc." I sensed we were heading into dangerous territory. I could smell it the way a rabbit knows a dog is nearby.

"That's great. So, what do you do?" she asked.

"I'm a therapist."

"You must love it. What kind of therapy?"

This is a loaded question. She's probably been in a ton of therapy herself.

"Well, basically psychodynamic. I used to work with addictions, but now I'm focusing on grief counseling. It's a different way of working. I have a pretty small practice."

Now I'm about to step out onto the ledge, the one that is about 30 stories above street-level. If only there was someone to talk me down.

"I'm also working on a book." I felt the need to justify my existence if my private practice is not full-time. *Big mistake here!* "I'm still on the first draft."

"What's it about?"

"It's a memoir." That's all I wanted to offer, hoping that would satisfy her curiosity.

"I've been thinking it's the time of my life to write a memoir. Just not exactly sure what I would write about yet."

"Well, sometimes you have something terrible happen which forces you to write about it." What the hell am I doing? I must be insane, testing to see how close to the brink I can go without falling.

She didn't ask me what happened.

"So do you have any other children?" she asked.

Here it is. The crossroads, the tipping point. Do I lie about Spencer's very existence? I can't do that. Cowardly. And it would be denying that he ever lived. I can't negate him like that.

"I have a son."

"Where is he? Is he in school?"

Here it is. The pause that seals my fate.

"*Well ...* he's no longer alive."

"Oh, I'm so sorry," she winced. "That's terrible."

"Yeah, it's hell. If you're a parent."

"I can't imagine." She looked down, shaking her head.

"Yeah, you don't want to. It's total hell. You don't want to live."

"If anything ever happened to either of my children…"

she whispered, still looking down.

"I didn't think I could survive it, either, but I did. It helped to write my book. And I found an incredible writing teacher. Her own daughter was murdered."

"Oh, God! That's terrible!"

"It is. It's a total nightmare. She went on to write an incredible book of poems about it. Absolutely earth-shattering. It won a bunch of prizes."

"I just don't get it."

"Yeah, neither do I. You just have to appreciate every single minute you have with your children. That's all you have."

"This just makes me worry more about them."

"Well, my son taught me that's a giant waste of time. Because then you're missing out on what you have right now."

She wanted to share her own experience. "There was this friend of my daughter's—not a close friend—he died of a brain tumor."

"Oh, dear. That's terrible. His poor family, and his friends."

"It was awful… How did your son die?"

"He was born with a heart defect. It was really complicated. I always knew he wasn't going to live to be 80 years old, but I had no clue he would die at 21. It was a complete shock. Totally unexpected. We thought he was going to be transferred to a hospital in Boston for surgery."

She wiped the tears dribbling down her cheeks. *She's got a heart*, I thought.

"This is our stop. You getting off here too?" she asked.

"Yeah. I live in Bucks County."

As the train slowed as it approached our station, I

wanted to say something like, "Too bad you're going back to Vancouver in eight days, because I'd ask if you want to meet for lunch." She had engaged with me about my dead son. That took some courage on her part.

I tried to catch her eye as the train came to a full stop, but she and her husband hopped up simultaneously and scurried to the rear of the car. I watched them quickly disappear into the parade of passengers exiting the train headed for the parking lots.

My heart sank. I felt ashamed for giving up so much of my grief to her. I reminded myself: *You're a walking advertisement:* MY CHILD DIED, AND YOUR CHILD COULD DIE, TOO.

On the drive home, I admonished myself: Remember this the next time you're tempted to share with strangers. Don't go out on that ledge. Keep the windows closed, dammit.

FOR DAYS AFTERWARDS, I THOUGHT ABOUT THE WOMAN on the train. I remembered my own callousness in years past. I had been not very different from her. Perhaps even worse.

Back in the Eighties, when I lived in Los Angeles, I got a phone call while preparing for a dinner party I was hosting later that evening. It was Father Fred, from our church in Santa Monica, letting me know that our dynamic young choir director Bruce had died very suddenly. I was stunned. He was so young! So creative! We all adored him! Should I cancel the party?

I wanted to, but I went ahead with it. Most everyone at the party was from our church and we all knew Bruce, but I never mentioned his death, and neither did anyone else. But I was thinking of Bruce the entire time.

After almost all the guests left, I pulled aside my closest friend Freddie. "Did you hear about Bruce? He had a heart attack!"

"Yes, I know." She looked at me, her face wincing with pain.

"He was so young! And he just got married! It's unbelievable." We shared our shock and sadness, hugging and crying together.

What was I thinking that I couldn't bring it up at the party? I remembered now. I thought I would somehow usher in a cloud of gloom over our fun. Instead it could have brought us closer together, to share our common love for our friend, an exceptionally talented musician. My ignorance.

A woman I once worked with, Ann, lost her husband at a young age, and I let too much time slip by before sending her a card or calling her, and remained silent, too embarrassed to acknowledge my neglect. I ran into her months later in a local shop, where she let me have it. "How could you not even write me? What is the matter with you? Why couldn't you call me?"

"I don't know… I'm so sorry," I replied, deeply ashamed. I had no defense whatsoever. I knew I was wrong.

I can look back and say to myself, I was young then, naïve, self-absorbed, busy with my young daughter. But those are lame excuses. It was my fear and ignorance which kept me silent.

What horrifies me the most is what I said at the funeral of the woman who had been my ex-husband's partner for years and a caring "step-mother" to my children. During the service, her brother reminisced about their carefree childhood summers at the Jersey Shore. Afterwards at the reception in their cousin's home, I approached Martin to offer my condolences. "You have some beautiful memories."

"Yeah, but I don't want memories—I want *her!*" he snapped.

I was startled, not anticipating his angry reaction. Now I totally got it. Of course he didn't want memories! Memories are hollow substitutes for the real thing, the flesh and blood human being you love and adore.

Now I knew: There is no fucking consolation.

PERHAPS NOW THAT I HAD PLUMBED THE DEPTHS OF Hell, I was capable of redemption. A friend who moved away emailed me about her colleague who had recently lost a college-age daughter. Would it be okay if she emailed me? "Of course," I answered. "I'm sure she is in a horrible, horrible place."

A few days later the woman wrote me, describing how she couldn't go to work, couldn't function, couldn't think of anything but her 21-year-old daughter who had died only three months before. She wanted to die.

"I know," I wrote back. "I wanted to die, too."

In dozens of emails over weeks and months she shared the details of her daughter's brief life, and the lack of support from her siblings and parents. Her daughter was one of triplets, and she worried about how her other two daughters were dealing with their sister's death. She never mentioned exactly how her daughter had died, and I never asked. I imagined she might have taken her own life. Her daughter was gone forever, and that was all that mattered now.

I knew there was nothing I could say to make it better.

Nothing. She knew that I got it. That was all I had to give. Just my willingness to listen to her anguish, her yearning for her beloved child, her boundless pain and suffering.

Even though we never had the opportunity to meet each other in person, we became friends. Almost two years after she first emailed me, she wrote,

> The thing I want to say to you Penny is, thank you so much. I don't know how you ever found the strength to deal with me in the beginning. I don't know if I could have made it without you. I know we never met. But you understood in ways no one else did and held out a lifeline, said things no one else knew to say. You are brave and I am just so grateful. I can't imagine what that took from you. Thank you.

I wrote her back:

> I always considered it an honor that you reached out to me, a stranger. It is just the worst hell in the world and no one else can possibly ever begin to grasp the depth of suffering and agony after your child has died. So you are almost at the two-year mark now? I remember hearing someone say at a seminar on grieving that the third year is the worst, and I thought, "So that's why I am still such a mess!" It actually helped me to hear that, but I've heard others get angry because they want to feel better. Feeling better was just never my goal, because I knew that my heartbreak was the measure of how much I loved my son. I always knew I would miss my son forever and the pain would never go away, just become an integral part of who I am and who I would be.

The leader of the Compassionate Friends meeting I used to attend would say that the vast majority of people, if caught in a burning building, will run out as fast as possible. But there are some very unusual individuals who run *INTO* the burning building. They are the heroes, the first responders. Disregarding their own safety, their mission is to rescue the people inside, as many as they can find. Very few people ever become firefighters, and most choose not to, but that's what I want to be now. A firefighter. I hope I have the guts and the strength to become a good one.

Jacob Stover

Prosymnus & Mnemosyne

powerless in the face of an immutable presence
knowing only orders of magnitude
yet having nothing to categorize this greatness

this vastness, yawning out beyond the limits of
    perception
a barometric cavern, breathing just as we do
infinite light, set dim, sometimes rising to a new apex
then receding again

during the high tide you can feel the ionic mist
beckoning your cells to leave the fold
innards churning and regenerating to emulate this astral
    sea

heart in my bowels,
cajoled by kind daemons,
I step out into the water

it neither parts
nor envelopes

rather it remains still,
it is undisturbed by my presence,
I am a quantity too thin and restless to wake it.

Kirk S. Westphal

Starting Again

A room dispossessed of its belongings
is perhaps as it should be

> The sculptor's hands see the body
> not the clothing

How unlike us it is,
returning to the nakedness of birth

> A lump of clay
> so malleable, a form within a cube, again

The everything of nothing yet
except the apple blossom

> to be formed by carefully removing
> unused space

Geometry of emptiness may be the only
perfection worth improving

> in an old and empty house I see
> its rooms, proud of their bodies.
> I, the sculptor.

Melissa Fournier

At Seven Years

for Camille

I watch you from the kitchen window—
white jacket, blue mittens.
You track simple words into snow,
duck beneath the playscape
pretending it's a home.
You're ghostly as you run
from mulberry to pine, rabbit-quick.
I won't say that a jay alights on a branch,
that your knock at the French door
leaves a mess of snow
dripping
down the glass,
or that at seven years, you make believe
the yard is the Arctic
where you're stranded on your own.
In some other place
all of this is true.
Here, I stand at the window
remembering the hour we lost you
in that freezing white room.

Lisa Burris

Fourteen Springs

M y son, Dylan Tyler Forsyth, died from a congenital diaphragmatic hernia at twenty-two days of age. What follows are a series of journaled pieces written on the anniversary of his birth. Each piece is relatively recent. I wrote very little in the years following his death, but perhaps healing came with the writing. Dylan was born on April 22, 2003; he died May 14th of the same year. He has been missed ever since.

Year Seven

The smell of medication and soap has triggered memories for years now. How I longed to feel your chest rising and falling against mine on your own accord. Your thick brown hair as it fell over your ears in long wisps framing your bloated face. Blood-covered baby blankets and the tubes and machines that lent you life. The words from picture books and whispered lullabies floating through a darkened room full of strangers. The hopeful, exhilarating, devastating rollercoaster that was your life. You were my first-born, and have since become my what-could-have-been. This story, the most worthy of my life, I've told over and over again, but it always ends the same. I'm the invisible mother and you're an unviable child. I'm desperate to rewrite the ending. For years I've teetered between *miraculously okay* and *completely unstable*; the line between the two is fine.

I remember the walk home the day I learned of you, my feet like lead on the sidewalk. Your existence brought chaos to my mind. I lay awake in my dorm room night after night, dreaming of ways to make you vanish. I was without bravery, finances or an education, questioning my ability to parent you. When I learned you'd be born sick, I was given the opportunity to terminate. It's easy to want what you won't be able to have. I chose your life, but have wondered if I wished your death. I'm still not sure.

You spent twenty-two days in an incubated prison, unable to breathe on your own. Your organs smothered each other; you flatlined twice. I never changed your diaper or saw your bare back. I left your side only to empty my breasts of milk which I accumulated like ounces of hope. I didn't hold you until you were taking your final breaths. Photographs from that day show your color changing from pale pink to grey-blue over a series of minutes. To this day, the thought of your spending your life without a hug sends me into a downward spiral. The truth is, I didn't have an option to choose and I wouldn't wish this outcome on my worst enemy. They day you died I emptied the milk from the freezer with vengeance, bag after bag of nourishment for a life thrown away.

Every 51 weeks spring rains arrive and I crumble to my knees. I'm suspended in time between all I've lost and all I have. My mind goes blank. I'm unable to sleep; my eyes swell, revealing my thoughts. My husband and three small children are life vests keeping me afloat. The buds pop, the flowers bloom, the world continues spinning. I'm surviving.

Your little sister asks why I left you at the hospital. I remind her that your body is buried beneath the creaky cedar at the edge of the wood.

I never raised you to look in awe at the world around you. I didn't teach you the value in small pleasures. You didn't know the value of healing relationships. You didn't learn that the most beautiful flowers blossom after they are drenched in storm water. You taught me every life lesson there was to learn. As your still, stiff little body lies in a grave, I've grown up.

Year Thirteen

We left the park with cold feet and worsening coughs. Sullen spirits turned as we headed to town for birthday pie. It was just far enough from closing time to not feel guilty about entering. I chose cherry crumb. The kids took a large table near the window; we filled all the chairs but one. I laid my pack on the floor so the chair would remain empty. As we sang "Happy Birthday" I avoided eye contact, staring at the table. For everyone else's birthday, we smile with our entire faces as our eyes dance around the table.

The kids sang their school style chant "Are you one? Are you two?... Are you thirteen?"

"Is he in heaven?"

"Is he alive under the earth?"

"Is he here with us right now?"

I don't know. My baby would be a teenager. I am a year further from my child. A grey-haired woman at a nearby table kept flashing smiles our way, her mind no doubt in another place, perhaps missing her own family. I'm sure from across the room we appear to be celebrating a living person. A glass of water was spilled; I was patient; I grabbed a rag. I thanked the earth for my children who bump their cups.

Teenagers flooded the joint moments before closing. They used the bathroom, didn't make a purchase, and left out the backdoor. I'm certain one of them must have been thirteen. I held back tears for other mothers' long-haired sons.

If you'd hugged me today, I would have cried. I counted my mere ability to dress and smile as a win. I avoided venturing too deep. I kept envisioning a day twelve and a half years ago.

I see myself in my dark living room. The shades are drawn; it could be night or day. I'm sobbing; I can't stop. My whole body shakes for hours. I choke on my own snot and spit. I cannot be consoled. I hate my baby-bearing body and my empty arms; I am not sure if I can face tomorrow.

I shake the thought, coming back to present day.

I'm in a place I never dreamed I'd be. My heart is at ease. I have healed in time. I am proud of my strong mind and body. I mark my progress—and vulnerability—on this day. April 22, 2016: On this Earth Day birthday, I am Dylan's mother, thirteen years out, still mourning the loss of my son.

Year Fourteen

I recently visited a hospital for a routine situation which required some additional attention. I'd postponed scheduling and considered canceling the appointment. I still envision death down each long corridor, behind every privacy curtain. I know this isn't rational, but I don't like hospitals.

I sat there uneasily, sweating through my shirt while I constantly reassured myself that I was capable of handling the situation. It's only a building.

The tall, quirky doctor who sat opposite me reviewed my family medical history. "What kind of cancer did your brother have?" he asked, and, "How long has your mother had diabetes?"

Then: "It says here you experienced a loss. Miscarriage?"

My head dropped to my feet; my heart followed. I was without an escape. I dryly swallowed. "No, sir," I said. "Diaphragmatic hernia."

"How long did the baby live?"

"Twenty-two days."

"I'm sorry. I don't know how anyone ever gets over that."

"Thank you. I guess I just never will."

"No, I guess you never could. So hard. I'm sorry."

I glanced up. Wavering, heavy droplets clung to the shaking rims of my eyes, but I didn't cry. Strength comes in many forms.

April showers: satisfying, quenching, soul-soaking rain. In the twenty-two days from late April to mid May the external world cycles from cold and dead to alive and blossoming; over those twenty-two days I relive life and death. I experience the thaw, I notice the melt; thick mud sticks to my thoughts. I pour myself into my living children. I work overtime at my job. Spring birds call out in song. I stand barefoot and threadbare with an armful of daffodils, sunshine on my shoulders.

Fourteen years is a long time. I'm proud of both my progress and my regression. So many of these days have both bright sunlight and pounding rains. Death is as natural, whole and fervent as life. Spring has finally arrived and has once again caught me off guard. I look around. I find my stride amongst the puddles. I journey on. I anticipate and celebrate, this day and tomorrow and the next, all that is and all that could not be. Until my dying day, I revisit his grave to plant color, rejoicing in dread and humbly embracing the spring.

Kathryn Holl

Your Shoes

I loved opening your closet, a world
kept hidden most of the time.
I was so small it was hard to reach the crystal knob,
    make the hard turn
to the right, listen for the metal release of the lock in the
    door jam,
the solid wood door opening to the magical world of
    your shoes.
I stole over to the shiny light blue pair,
toe-less, single back strap, sparkling.
I slid off my red Keds, stripped off my anklets, tossing
    them aside
as one would an unwanted tissue.
I moved the shoes near the wall, balancing as I stepped
    in, first one foot
then the other.
I stood tall, feeling at once transported to that grown-up
    world
where I could be beautiful and be heard.

Clip, clop out of the closet, steadying myself on walls
    and door jams
into the sun where the shoes sparkled brightly
and I reigned queen.
When you died the shoes were gone.
My feet too big now to fill your shoes.
Still I reach, trying hard to open the door to the world
    where
I can be beautiful and be heard.

Anne-Marie Oomen

Ten Primaries

1. Birds, genus of hover and wing, descend from a previous eon of dinosaurs. After the meteor, it took them untold millennia to evolve flight; hollow-boned miniatures of their once great physicality, the mutancy of genes splaying out feathers more beautiful with each evolutionary spiral. Eventually, eagles evolved ten primaries on each wing. I want to believe we are like that, that we still evolve.

2. Bees see the world of flowers like landing on a runway in the dark, in glowing ultraviolets, guiding them to their work. They see what we cannot, what is invisible to us, that far end of the spectrum. And what humans see is barely visible to them. They bungle forward, lacking apparatus, sometimes hurting themselves. I was like that, lacking apparatus to see ultraviolet, landing in grief light…

3. …because as my father lay dying on a perfect day in June, he had not made nor could he express any clear wishes. I made choices that led to his death. The death was inevitable, but the choices were not, nor were they made in wisdom. Rather, blooming panic. After, here is me winging into a world I could not see properly, not even the world that I was assigned, familiar with. I had

the physical apparatus, but bumped my way down a strange runway with only blurred lights.

4. As a species, we don't see much of afterlife. We allure ourselves with ego, dominance, self-superiority, false haloes, so-called everlasting souls. We forget: we are one species among many. Animal also. To what do we rise?

5. I'm not denying soul; but might soul's nature be floral? Blooming and fading, with colors that only bees, birds, certain children, the dying can see? Oh, a few of our species may have partial apparatus for such things. We call them prophets. They point to the unseen, partially seen, rarely seen. Sometimes they pose as therapists.

6. When did the bird sign first appear? My friends say it happened at the burial site, that while I was reciting prayers, tending my mother and sisters, and my eyes were pulled earthward to see the coffin lowered—some mourners heard a cry and looked up, saw a kestrel hover above the grave. Some said it hovered for a long time; others said it swooped away and returned again and again. After, when I heard the story, the first word to rise was *guide*; the second, *messenger*.

7. Then, the eagles rose. In the days after his funeral, they came to us, or so it seemed: huge things on dark

wings, primary, crowned in white: that much we could see. Mature and high flying, hunting, scanning, they suddenly swooped, following my sisters and me down the lonely beach where we walked arm in arm, crying softly. Their cries, like a scream, but not fearful, more… confident, like calling a name. More sightings, uncannily often. We saw them land in open fields, streak over grassy meadows, ride the thermals off high bluffs. My sister texts from Colorado. *Mountain pass. Eagle overhead.* Me from Boston: *Eagle over quad, carrying prey.*

8. Months after, the grief therapist said I needed to integrate his death into my world view—to add that color. He made me tell my father's death story again and again. With his help, I grew pin feathers, seeing each glow in the dark, still encased in keratin sheath. I felt lightness but not strength, a hand with fingers that finally learn not what to do, but how to feel forward by touch.

9. A necessary skepticism. It's easy to see eagles: populations on the rise all over the country. We walk where they hunt: beaches, passes, gorges with updrafts. Though my father did revere them as the country's bird and as skilled predators, they are not my father's

new form. But how do these winged creatures, being eons old, see us? Did they see the colors of his longing and answer? The bird-sign happened more than chance allowed.

10. Even today, long after, it goes on, over and over, bird-sign/dadsign. Each time the winged eagles rise, I think ultraviolet: what is the message, the guidance? There, but I cannot see it. Here in the meteoric universe, these hands—ten primaries—shape my incomplete vision out of dark wings, and I dream the not-yet-visible flights all around us, fierce and ultraviolet.

Melissa Seitz

There Will Be Birds

1988: Fatly pregnant and exhausted after my second ultrasound in two days, I walked through a labyrinth of hallways in the Midland hospital, guided by a woman who had no idea what to say to me. Sunlight warmed the glass and shadows of light played our silhouettes off of each other against indifferent walls and office doors. Outside, in the crisp January air, nuthatches, chickadees, and blue jays sought shelter in the small bushes and trees gracing the hospital grounds.

The silent woman walked me through my doctor's waiting room as if leading a parade. Other pregnant women looked up at me and smiled, comrades with bellies in various stages of pregnancy, before quickly looking down at their roundness underneath layers of sweaters and bras that no longer fit quite right. The terror on my face muted a room filled with hope.

The woman seated me in a comfortable chair in my doctor's office and quickly retreated through the door. I thought of my son and husband, and their upcoming weekend trip to celebrate my son's sixth birthday. I had been looking forward to two days of sleeping, reading, and rubbing lotion on my continually expanding stretch marks.

The doctor walked in, sat down across from me, and

cleared his throat as he placed a folder on top of the desk. I looked away from him and scanned the pictures of wild animals on his office walls. As if I had been invited for tea, I wanted to ask him if he had been on safari. Instead, I refocused. I knew he had to ruin my life.

"Is your husband with you?"

"At work. Just tell me what you have to say."

"We should call him," he offered.

"Tell me," I said. Without flinching, as if I had already taken the blow, I locked my eyes on him. I was the hunter.

He realized that I refused to give him an alternative. "Your baby has anencephaly."

I was a spelling bee champ, a lover of language, but I did not know this word. He defined it, clinically, in a monotone of sadness and weariness. The words "incomplete skull, undeveloped brain," and "not viable" rang out and stung my ears. I fell forward, wrapped my arms around my belly as if I could save my daughter from her destiny. My heart began to break, piece by piece, exploding into my belly. "Yes, I should call Jim," I said. "How will I tell Matt? He's almost six."

The doctor handed me the phone, but I did not hear what he said as I dialed the number for Jim's office. Jim answered on the first ring.

"The baby is going to die. She is going to die." I hung up the phone and waited for him to come and get me. I could feel Nicole move inside of me. I rubbed my hands in a circular motion around her, as if we were both swimming in circles, our bodies forever reaching for what we could not have.

§   §   §

NICOLE ENTERED THIS WORLD ON FEBRUARY 22ND, 1988, and left us on February 26th. Four days merged into hospital surrealism where my son brought hand-drawn cards for me and stared at Nicole. Nicole wore knitted hats around her head as if warding off the cold. I did not tell Matt that the hats protected Nicole's incomplete skull. Her hands, fingers, body, and face were perfect. She reminded me of songbirds I had tried to save over the years after unfortunate collisions with the living room or kitchen windows. They did not see their reflection; rather, they faced death an instant before it happened.

When I looked into the mirror at the hospital before I left to head home, I wondered who the woman was staring back at me. Soon, I would have my 33rd birthday, but I did not recognize this woman, her face drowning in grief, her eyes painted red with sorrow. I remember touching the mirror lightly as if to reassure myself that I was alive. As Jim, Matt, and I left the hospital that day, we were all given something to carry. I held a vase full of heartbreak flowers while the February wind signaled its apathy.

WE WERE A SMALL GROUP AT THE MIDLAND CEMETERY for Nicole's funeral. A blanket of snow covered the ground and the gravestones in the children's section. My father and mother, barely rested after a series of flights from Dodge City, Kansas, stood on one side of me. Jim's parents, in town from Farmington Hills, stood next to him. Our neighbors, Vicki and Bill, joined the circle with the men from the funeral home. I had explained what would happen at the funeral to Matt, and I asked him if he wanted to come with us. For some reason, and I do not remember why, it was important to me that I give him this choice—maybe I thought I could protect him. He chose not to come.

A FEW DAYS AFTER THE FUNERAL, JIM RETURNED TO work, and Matt headed back to school. I was alone, and the hallway in our home became my sanctuary. My breasts finally stopped producing milk for Nicole. The scar from my C-section seemed to vibrate when I ran my fingers across the seam.

Reluctant to stay in bed and afraid to go outside, I sat in the hallway with my back against one wall and my feet resting against the molding on the opposite side. From this vantage point I could not see the living room or the kitchen. The bathroom door, the door to our bedroom, and the door to Matt's room were safe. The room that would have been Nicole's was just out of view; a slight bend in the hallway prevented me from seeing the door. No one could see if I was home; I could not see outside. We had no pictures on the walls. I felt imprisoned in my self-made coffin, but at least I could breathe. The hardwood floor underneath me at least felt like solid ground. I felt weightless, a hummingbird landing on a barely visible branch.

When school let out for the summer, Matt played with the neighborhood children, and we spent a lot of time going up to our cottage at Higgins Lake. Our close friends at the time had a place across the lake from us, and I finally went to visit them one day. Their daughter Laura had been born in May. In December of 1987, Beth and I had sat just feet apart on my living room couch, our bellies glowing with life, as she tried to teach me how to knit. I never learned. On a hot summer day in 1988, Beth walked me to Laura's room, where she was sleeping. I screamed and ran out of the house. It would be a long time before I could be in the presence of babies without weeping.

I could not bear to have Matt out of my sight. When school started again that fall, I began volunteering at the school library. Matt's first-grade teacher gave me simple jobs in the classroom, and I helped children cut up paper pumpkin decorations for Halloween and turkeys for Thanksgiving. The school librarian asked me to help shelve books and do other organizational tasks in the library.

One day, as I stood in the library at Chippewassee School, a woman from my neighborhood walked by in the hallway. She had already managed to get my son uninvited from a neighborhood birthday celebration because she had been "concerned," as she said, that our grief "might upset the other children." Instead of waving at me in the library, she frowned and kept walking. I felt naked, as if my heartache were on display, pulsing with neon lights.

The next day at school, the librarian and the first-grade teacher swore me to secrecy before telling me my neighbor had complained to the principal that I should not be in the library, since I might upset the children while shelving books. The teacher and the librarian had been appalled; they convinced the principal that I should be hired to work in the library instead. I began receiving a paycheck, and whenever I got the chance, I smiled at the woman who was so frightened of my grief.

As I continued negotiating the world outside of the hallway of our house, I became restless. Although my body was fully healed from having a C-section for Nicole, my heart and soul needed a lot of repairing. A friend, an avid runner, suggested I try running.

I owned a pair of Adidas running shoes. They were

awkward and clunky, but they fit me perfectly. One day while Jim was at work and Matt was at school, I put on a pair of exercise shorts and ran/walked the 1.4 miles around my subdivision. I did not die.

The next day, I went outside again. I begin listening to the birds chirping in the woods filling our neighborhood landscape, a landscape so foreign to my mother who grew up in Kansas that the trees made her claustrophobic. I convinced myself the birds were cheering me on, so I greeted them with a "hello, bird" every chance I could. My voice reminded me of the mourning doves cooing at the base of our birdfeeders in the spring.

In time, I ran around the entire subdivision without stopping. I wondered what it was like out on the country roads, all paved, that I was used to driving on when I returned from Matt's school or grocery shopping. I began to experiment, and I began running longer distances. People waved from their cars at me. Mr. Albee, a neighbor who lived about a quarter mile from me, clapped for me whenever I passed his house. Another neighbor suggested I run through his sprinklers on a hot day. Their kindness overwhelmed me.

My parents came to visit for a few days during the holidays. My mother and I were washing dishes in the kitchen one afternoon, and I started singing a silly song, something she and I always did when I was growing up. She looked at me, and tears sprang from her eyes.

"What's wrong?" I asked.

"I think you're going to be okay," she said.

We looked at each other, and I imagined her scars and my scars melting into one. She was never able to have children, and they adopted me when I was two months old. I realized her heartbreak shouldered an even heavier weight when Nicole died.

AS A WAY TO MANAGE MY ANGER AT THE WORLD, AND MY fear of not being with Matt every moment of every day, I began running even longer distances, and I competed in road races: 5ks, 10ks, 8-milers, 10-milers, half marathons. With running, I felt free from all sorrow and heartache in a way that nothing else could fix. Even the occasional mishap, such as the time I tripped and fell over a branch in the road, taught me something about myself. That day, as I sat on the cold November pavement examining my ripped pants, bloodied knee and embedded gravel visible through my torn running pants, I knew I had to pick myself up and somehow make my way home. I refused to call Jim and ask for help. A pileated woodpecker, from his perch high above me in an oak tree, laughed in his signature "wuk, wuk, wuk" to remind me to get up and get moving. The one-mile walk home, painful and filled with a lot of swearing and tears, reminded me that I was very much alive. The scar on my knee is a constant reminder.

THIS YEAR WOULD HAVE BEEN NICOLE'S 30TH BIRTHDAY, and I found myself mired in sadness and fear. Over the years, I had become used to my trips to the cemetery alone. I needed my time alone with Nicole. I kept my heartache close; only close friends and family knew Nicole's story.

The day before Nicole's birthday, I drove down to Midland so that I could spend the night at Matt's house. My dear friend Darcy and her two-year-old daughter, Hadley, picked me up to drive us south of town to search for snowy owls. I felt such peace and joy in those moments as we spotted owls and shot photographs. Later, after they dropped me off at Matt's house, I wrote a poem for Nicole before he came home from work.

The next morning, long after Matt had headed off to work, I drove to the Midland Cemetery, less than two miles from Matt's house. With a small brown basket and a bouquet of tulips, I parked and walked towards her gravestone. Since I had been taking sunrise pictures for many months without missing a day, I knew that I would take a very different kind of sunrise picture on her birthday.

After taking my sunrise picture of Nicole's grave, I asked Nicole what she thought I should do. I struggled with the idea of posting something on Facebook, but I felt as if I needed to share my grief.

I waited. Chickadees in the distance chirped at me as if echoing my doubts. A light wind rustled the branches of naked tree limbs. I ran my hand across her name, engraved on the pink headstone: NICOLE CHANTELLE SEITZ. I drove back to Matt's and loaded my few pictures on my iPad. I pulled up my poem and read it one more time.

I placed a singular picture on Facebook along with the poem I had written for Nicole. I had decided it was time to publicly share my grief. I pressed "Share" and got up to make some tea.

February

I remember this:
My daughter is dead.
Nicole is in a white coffin,
and my grief covers her body.
My husband floating in air towards me.
My son, six years old, safe and warm at a friend's house.

I need to get back to him. Hold him close.
He chose not to come to this funeral.
How does one decide these things at six?
How did I discuss this with him?
Burying my face in the warmth of my father's wool coat.
My mother's face shattering into a thousand fragments
of light.
Our best friends and my husband's parents standing in the
shadows of our misery.
A man from the funeral home telling me it is time to leave.

But I have never left that day behind me.
It follows me wherever I go.
For thirty years, I have hated the month of February.
The killer of dreams.
A basket of broken hearts.

AFTER DRINKING MY TEA, I PUT ON MY RUNNING SHOES
and dressed for the weather. I went for a short walk in Matt's
neighborhood. I thought of Jim and Matt and how we now
travel to races together. Matt runs road races with me, and
after the races, we share stories of road hogs (people who
run in large groups blocking the road-race course), people
wearing the race shirt on the day of the race (a big no-no),
or less-than optimal road-race conditions (icy roads, high
winds, or pouring rain). We always find a local restaurant,
eat a meal, drink a few beers, and hit the road in search of
ice cream. Then we figure out where our next race will be.

There is no endpoint for this loss, this continual story of
"what might have been" playing through my head, especially
when I see young women who are around the same age that
Nicole would be. I am like a bird on a wire, watching and
waiting for the right moment to fly into the brilliant sky.

Chaunie Brusie

This Is Love

He calls to check on me, the sounds of four children screeching in my ear, even over the speaker of the phone. His voice is on edge, as it always is when they are in their hyper mood, but it softens when he asks me how I'm doing, if I need anything. I hesitate before answering him, not wanting to bring him into the world of women, but I am bleeding our baby away and I don't want to go to the store.

"I'll get the pads," he says. "I'll get anything you need."

This is love.

She hands it to me, the brushed glass purple, stuck still with the particles of the sand she dug it up from. She has watched me hide my tears this week, she has blinked away her own, not understanding but knowing enough to realize her mama is hurting. And she has kept it, this token all day long, waiting, bursting to give it to me. When she does, I think it is the most beautiful thing I have ever seen, this dollar store trinket buried and forgotten in a sandbox, a butterfly resting perfectly in my palm.

"I got this for you, Mom. I wanted you to have it."

This is love.

Greta Bolger

El Fin del Dia de los Muertos

Today I take down the altar, wrap and box up
the fragile Katrina, still intact after all these years
except for a few broken fingers. Today, I gather

the yellow silk flowers, put to bed the sugar skull,
the sugar basket of food and drink for the dead,
lay down the purple and yellow candles,

return memorial photos to their mourners,
carefully lay to rest the papel, multicolored Mexican
tissue paper laser cut into skeletons

of various ways of living—a man in a top hat,
a little girl in pigtails, this thin paper precious to me,
irreplaceable now as they are, my two unforgotten sons.

Julia Brabenec

On a Fall Day

Searching out the space where your ashes
and my bones shall spend eternity—deciding
what to put in place to mark the spot—several
tiny firs appeared nearby, like volunteers to join
the plan. Yes, they will nicely guard our mound.
Of course, there must be lilacs, too, and since
they need some ash to sweeten up the ground,
I know that yours will surely do.

But on a day like this there isn't any
thought of hurrying. The sound
of southbound geese, so joyful in their race
from winter's breath, satisfies my heart with
grateful peace—no space for thoughts of death.
Only that I yearn to do the math, carry out the plan,
point out the path to where, beside your urn, my
body wants to lie when it runs out of breath.

Mary Robertson

The Coat

There is a coat drive taking place in my town. Bins are groaning with contributions, but I still know that my closet holds items that need to be donated. I carefully fold a few old jackets of mine and a lovely little fur stole my girls wore ages ago with their fancy Christmas dresses. Then it is time for the big decision.

The only item of my late husband Tom's clothing that I have not been able to give away or repurpose is his dress overcoat. It's a funny, huge thing, sized extra-large although he really wasn't, bought from Eddie Bauer decades ago and still in perfect shape: gray and brown tweed with a brown leather collar and buttons. He wore it to church and any other dress-up winter occasion, and just looking at it conjures the image of him in an instant. When we met he had been away from church for many years, but no matter how many times I said I was fine going alone, and despite his great fondness for a long, slow wake up on the weekends, he always said, "I want to go." And often that meant wearing the big overcoat.

Maybe because it is such an unusual item, or because no male friend or relative wants it, or because I can still picture him wearing it—for whatever reason, it is still hanging in the front hall closet nine months after he died.

Winter is coming and someone could be kept very warm by that coat. Tom would want someone to enjoy its warmth, I am sure of that.

But as I fold it and start to put it in the bag I hold it close and speak out loud to Tom, telling him how much I miss him, all the specific things I miss about him, how much I wish he was still here to wear the coat, but how now it is time for me to pass it on.

Today I delivered the bag of coats to the Recreation Center. I liked picturing a little girl in the stole, a thinner, younger woman than I in my jackets, and some man, whose face I can't quite see, smiling at the handsome tweed and heavy warmth of Tom's old overcoat.

There is a scene toward the end of Puccini's opera *La Bohème* where one of Mimi and Rodolpho's artist friends sells his coat to raise money for the consumptive Mimi's medicine. They are freezing in a garret in Paris, and it is an act of pure sacrifice and love. He sings a beautiful aria to the coat, thanking it for all the warmth and comfort it has provided.

There is never a dry eye in the house.

Robb Astor

My Father's Field

when i find myself in a field of iris
amidst hues of yellow and purple
acres of green
up to my waist in inflorescence

when i know he's finally gone back to farming
that for all the years beyond the far side of death
he's done nothing except plant irises
in furrows once of corn

when the sun's setting fills the field with too rich a green
and the purple and yellow begin to burn
and i see these colors again in my father's eyes
i understand it is he who made it burgeon

when my knees and shoulders ache
and i'm bent down in dust
and my clothes are frayed
from all that's turned fallow and barren

when my knuckles are stiff
and i find full measure of welcome in his hands
calloused and split, broken with dirt
and the soil is fecund in spite of his death

when i see it was my father
who'd always cross over to me
but now it is i who have come to his farm of iris
i know he's prepared it just for this

but look—
my world begins to slink back in
the distant colors of the field start to waver
and only what is near remains

where irises still glower
where laden with flowers
their green stalks sway
and brush smooth against my cheeks

when i part the damp blades
i find only lichen
assuming the hollows
of his graven name

Angela Haase

We Know They Danced

After they picked up a pint of whiskey at Beulah Drug
my parents went to a dance at the White Owl.
Their first date, 1947. July and the air cooled.
The sky inked darker each hour and crooned.
They married that November.
When I was a kid, they'd pile us into the car
and head out to the B&L Bar for Friday fish fry
with dancing afterward. If we were good
we'd get a piece off the old man's plate.
If we were lucky my older sister would meet us
after work and let us stay two songs to watch them dance.
Then she'd drive us kids home in her Plymouth Fury.
I remember their coincidence, their grace—
their eventual twirl then dip. The music not bad
for locals at a small town roadhouse, biggest dance floor
around for miles. I remember reading about a stump
from a famed California Redwood that was bigger.
It was felled in 1852, planed into a smooth dance floor.
I wonder if it could grow back—that tree.
The stump is still there.
Imagine a Jack & the Beanstalk moment—
trunk popping and pushing skyward, branches then leaves
sprout as the whole tree shoots up. Dancers glide across
the years and the rings of the tree as it climbs, notes
of a waltz fading as it all rises into heaven.

Daniel W. Stewart

Flatbed

W hen the warning flashes on the dashboard, I know
what I ought to do.

The warning's language is technical and vague, but it's
amber and I know an emergency would be red. Still, the
exclamation point would normally give me pause. After
all, I'm only 100 miles into a 500-mile journey. The sensible
thing to do would be to go back home, fix the problem,
then start again. Tomorrow, maybe.

But I am not turning around. As the speedometer's
needle climbs to 70, I prop my phone on the steering wheel,
darting my eyes between road and screen as I search for the
warning's meaning. *Alternator,* one man reports. *Battery,*
says another.

Nobody says, *Emergency.*

I re-read the warning one more time, trying to gauge
my own sense of worry, but when I think about worst
cases, the car is not what comes to mind. When I saw the
warning, I was already awash in a sea of dread.

I keep driving. I'm rushing to get there in time, and I'm
worried I'm already late. I try not to think how little I'll be
able to do when I arrive. At least I'll be there, I tell myself.
At least I can witness what must be witnessed.

I'm driving to see my parents but I'm not driving to

their house. When I put my destination into the map, I typed its old name, the name I knew when I was growing up a few miles away: Mercy South. It's a hospital.

My mother called yesterday to let me know she had checked my father into the hospital, but I saw no reason to worry. After all, my father is often in the hospital these days. Ever since his open-heart surgery a dozen years ago, his ailments have multiplied—eyes, back, ankle, teeth, and now blood—and I've gotten use to thinking there is something called a "routine emergency." When a simple planned test turned into a hospital admission, I wasn't surprised. I can't make the long drive each time he goes to the hospital.

So as my mother gave me details, I nodded a little absently. His immune system wasn't responding after his latest round of chemotherapy, she said, and then she began to describe what she saw happening to his body. In the land of the sick, conversations are often detailed and biological. But then she said she'd seen something she'd never seen before. She'd heard about it, though. The same thing had happened with a sister and with a brother-in-law.

Both of them were dead within days.

My mother, even at age 77 and standing barely over five feet tall, has the toughness of someone who survived the Korean War as a child, and she was trying not to sound afraid now. But when I said, "I'll be there tomorrow," she didn't try to hide her relief.

So now I press the button on the dashboard that makes the warning go away. The car just needs to hold together and I'll arrive in seven hours, while it's still daylight.

Ninety minutes later, amid the thick, impatient traffic of the interstate between Detroit and Chicago, the warning reappears, and a few minutes later the ventilation system stops working. The engine is still running, though. I roll the windows down and keep driving—until the dashboard warning turns red, ordering me to find help immediately. It is, it seems, now an emergency. I make it to a rest area, where my car dies.

But I find help with a relative who lives half an hour away who helps me limp my car to her local mechanic—"he's honest," she says—and then drops me off at a rental-car counter. I put my bags in the trunk of a clean, factory-new car, turn my map back on, and resume the trip. I'll arrive after dark, but I'll be at the hospital today.

My father's room is down a short hallway from the bank of elevators. I stop to wash my hands, then to rub them with sanitizer. There's a sign on the door and I obey it, pulling a paper mask over my mouth. The door is wide and heavy when I open it.

My father is sitting in a chair next to the bed.

"Doesn't he look better?" my mother asks.

She's trying to sound cheerful, but my father looks terrible. The stoop of his once-broad shoulders has grown more pronounced, but what alarms me is the pallor of his skin, which is almost the color of the peeled-back white sheets of the hospital bed. The room, dim beneath a few indirect fluorescent lights, is a palette of blond woods and light grays. The only color in the room is the deep scarlet bag that's dropping blood into his vein.

"You look great," I lie, leaning over to hug him around the shoulder. Up close the coarse whiskers of his face are almost translucent. I see the now-familiar layer of fear in his eyes, but also relief. He looks terrible, but my father is still here.

We keep him upright for another half an hour—we've had many reminders about the dangers of hospital bed-sores—but then he's ready for sleep. We help maneuver him and his IV lines into bed, then I hug him again.

I follow my mother to their house, but when I wake up the next morning she's gone.

"I had a bad dream," she tells me over the phone. "Your father needed help and nobody was coming." She'd returned to the hospital to spend the night in the chair beside his bed, nodding off every now and again. "I'm used to it," she says.

I know it's impossible to get used to not sleeping, but I know what she means and don't argue.

My brother arrives a few hours later, after his own 300-mile drive north. I've been trying to be useful, fetching water, ice, snacks and other small, mostly useless comforts, but my brother—older than me, and a senior executive at an international company—is restless to take some positive action. He's focused on the hematologist/oncologist, the specialist in cancers that affect the blood. This doctor ordered the round of chemotherapy that's left our father anemic and immune system-compromised—the exact opposite of its supposed purpose.

"I think he caused this," my brother says.

The doctor agrees to meet with us at his small office in the hospital. When we arrive, he points us toward two small chairs. "Your father has done well," he begins, speaking quickly.

When I look at my brother, I think I see a mirrored expression of my own incredulity. Our father has a constant IV drip of blood, while also having blood drawn several times a day. It feels as if he's getting blood on a short-term loan.

"What happened?" my brother asks.

"I didn't know if I wanted to do this round of treatment," he says, "but your father wanted to give it a try."

"So the treatment failed."

The doctor shakes his head. "We began this treatment three and a half years ago," he says, and the treatment usually stops working after two years. His voice is unexpectedly cheerful. "Your father has been a great success!" He's not young but has an almost boyish grin.

Three and a half years. It seems longer than that since our father was diagnosed with a kind of cancer—it used to be called "pre-leukemia," although that's not quite accurate—that has no cure, at least for someone of his age. Forty months of chemotherapy, in occasional week-long treatments that left him depleted, had become part of a routine. What did it matter if he never got better if he never got noticeably worse?

It's one of the illusions, when you've crossed over into the land of the sick, to think that "stable" means "normal"—and that it can somehow last forever. Now the hematologist is telling us that the treatment worked for more than three years, and he's happy. We got more time than most, and *more time* was always the objective.

But when I look out the window behind the doctor, at the cars queuing at the stop sign to leave the hospital—it's a difficult turn; there ought to be a traffic signal there—I realize that I'd expected that *more time* would somehow go on forever.

In his room, sitting up in his bed, now with a second iv drip line in his arm, my father looks drawn. He's lost almost ten pounds in just a few days. "I want you two to know," he tells us, his voice reed-thin, "that I couldn't have asked for better sons."

I put my hand on his arm. His skin should be warmer. "You've been a great father," I say, but the complicated verb tense unsettles me. I want something simple, some language that doesn't spread across time, so I add, "You *are* a great father."

But the next day, somehow, we're preparing for his release. There's the expected paperwork and the routine hurry-up-and-wait for the approvals and medications and scheduling of home-care nursing visits. Again we see the hematologist, who has final authority for his release. "I want him to stay in the hospital," the doctor says, "but your father really wants to go home." He shakes his head a little as he signs the papers. My father was, more or less, stable again.

My mother, brother and I get him home, and we begin talking again about the future. Summer is ending. We'll gather again over Labor Day, we decide; I'll return with my wife, and my brother will bring his wife and two sons.

The crisis past, my brother heads home first. A few days later—a week after I arrived—I'm in my father's bedroom, hugging him goodbye. "We'll see you in ten days," I say.

My father keeps me in the hug. "I don't think I'll last that long," he says into my ear.

I pat his back until his arms relax again. "You're getting better," I say, not sure if I'm lying, or to whom. But, I remind myself, I'd come expecting the worst, and being able to say *see you later* is absolutely better than the worst.

When I settle back into the rental car, good news behind me for the drive home, the contrast with my earlier trip makes me feel almost ecstatic. I'm going home.

The only hiccup is that I need to pause about halfway

to retrieve my own car. The same relative meets me when I return the rental car and she drives me to her mechanic, who explains that he found the problem was the alternator—but he wasn't actually able to fix it. "I guess I don't have the tools to work on a German car," he explains apologetically, offering me the keys.

"Um—" I begin.

"The battery's good, though," he continues. "I gave it a full charge. That's probably good enough. Should be."

It's not the strongest vote of confidence, but I'm in too good of a mood to let the news bother me. The original dashboard warning reappears quickly, so when I stop for gas I call the nearest dealership. It's afternoon now, the mechanic tells me, so they wouldn't be able to get to my car before tomorrow. The fix might take until the day after.

"But it might last," I say into the phone, looking for good news. "I'm only 250 miles from home."

There's a pause I hear as a shrug. "Might," he says. "Might not, though."

I decide that two noncommittal answers equal a yes, so when my car starts, I pull back onto the highway and a few minutes later drive past the exit that would take me to the dealership. I want to be home, and I'm feeling lucky.

Three hours later I'm sitting on a bench seat, my feet on top of a tool box, as Roger, who is driving this tow truck, finishes chaining my car to the flatbed behind me. He climbs into the truck and turns the key in the ignition; the truck engine rattles to life and gives a barking cough as we pull across the road and back onto the highway.

Roger points to a hole in the dashboard. "No radio," he says, or rather shouts, because we're grinding slowly up to highway speeds with the windows down because there's no air conditioning, either. The truck gives guttural grunts, the chains holding my car rattle behind us, and the wind circles inside the cab with the force of a tropical storm. The truck sputters on uphill grades, slowing even as Roger downshifts from gear to gear, his foot heavy on the pedal. "It's an old truck," he shouts across to me.

Roger is a small, middle-aged man with a restless, nervous energy. We're driving northwest now, into the rose gold of the setting sun, as he recounts to me stories about his military service and his dozen years as a repo man around Detroit. His stories begin with unexpected phrases like, "The first time I got shot…"

I hadn't known that a derringer bullet feels like a bee sting while a crossbow bolt feels, as he says, "like a fucking crossbow." I didn't know there's a difference, legally, between breaking into a garage that's attached to a house versus one that's not.

But Roger's stories eventually slow down, and for a few minutes he goes silent before he says, "I talk a lot. I bet you wish we had a radio."

He's apologizing, which surprises me. I lean closer to his good ear, which is fortunately the one closest to me. "I like hearing your stories," I say, raising my voice amid the din. "I'm not talking because my voice doesn't carry through the noise." What I'm saying is true, but it's only the simplest part of the truth—the part I'm able to shout.

I'm still mostly listening when we clear a traffic circle and turn onto long stretch of road that leads to where he's doing to drop off me and my car. We're soon on a long uphill. The bass rumble of the engine replaces the wind noise as we slow, Roger grinding a gear when he downshifts. When a white sedan sticks close to our bumper, despite the empty passing lane, Roger waves his hand out the window. "Go around!" he yells. "Go around!" We reach the top of the hill, the grade flattens, and we begin to pick up speed again.

"Hey," Roger says again, "sorry I been talking the whole time. You must be glad we're almost there."

"I am," I say, but I don't know how to explain why. I barely know myself.

What Roger doesn't know is that, in the back of my car, which is now on the back of his truck, there is a garment bag holding a dark suit and a starched white shirt, as well as a cardboard box holding the shiny black leather shoes I've had for more than twenty years. These traveled with me from my car to the rental car, and then back into my car. Soon, after he slides my car into a spot at the repair shop, I'll move the suit into my wife's car and we'll take it back home.

I'd brought that suit and those shoes to wear to my father's funeral. On my drive south, through my car's (first) breakdown, I'd been hurrying to get where I did not want to go: my father's deathbed. I had carried the clothes I would wear to bury him, but now I'm carrying them back home, still in bag and box, unworn. My broken-down car is rattling atop an old flatbed tow truck with a worn-out engine, but I'm going back home and my father is still alive. He isn't well, and I know he will never be well again, but he is stable. The time we have left is not indefinite, but we are not yet at its end.

I don't yet know, riding in that tow truck, that the end will come in four months. Over Labor Day we'll buy my father a motorized recliner, to make him more comfortable and to lift the literal load on my mother. We'll spend Thanksgiving together, too. I'll come down again a week and a half before Christmas, to be there for my father's surgery, the one that will, we hope, begin patching up some of his ailments so he can actually begin improving. When things go awry, at first I won't be alarmed. I'll call my brother, reassuring him that he doesn't need to rush up—but a few hours later, I'll call again and say, *Come now.*

We'll bury my father before Christmas, and I won't be prepared: no suit, no shoes. When, in the midst of helping with burial arrangements, I'll have to shop for a black suit and black leather shoes, I'll think about those hours in the tow truck with Roger. I'll think about how *more time* is never *enough time.*

Because Roger already knew this truth. Beside me on the bench seat, talking over the noise and in between the funny stories and the odd ones, he also told me about his wife. She had brittle bones caused by a congenital and progressive disease, he said. They'd been able to have children, but as her health worsened and her bones grew fragile, she was forced eventually into a motorized wheelchair. They managed the occasional crisis, knowing she wasn't going to get better, but then things would get stable again.

The month before, Roger told me, his wife had been feeling good enough to travel by herself to visit family and friends a few states away. It was one of those family members who called him: the cause of death was a heart attack, he was told. She wasn't yet fifty.

"That's so young," I say, and as this man and I ride together, we let the noise mask the silence.

IT'S DARK AS WE MAKE THE SLOW, LABORED TURN INTO the auto shop driveway. I know that in a couple of days I'll get a repair bill steep enough that I'll reflexively do some quick math about the current value of my thirteen-year-old car. But I also know that when I look at that bill, I'll feel a kind of joy to have a problem whose solution is just money. I can see my wife's car in the parking lot, where she is waiting for me.

Early in our trip Roger said to me, *Nobody riding in a tow truck is having a good day*—but I am, and I didn't quite realize how good it was until I got into this tow truck. I began this journey expecting I would have to bury my father. A week later, he's still alive and he's home, and at the end of this unexpected journey I'll be home again, too.

I don't know how much time is left, only that it will not be enough because there can never be enough. I am coming home knowing that endings are inevitable, even if that knowledge isn't the same thing as acceptance and even if it won't protect me from sorrow. But I do think I understand that an ending does not mean there has been no success.

The truck is slowing and it's finally getting quiet. Roger is looking for a good place to winch my car down to the ground.

I don't know how to explain to him that I feel almost giddy, so I just lean toward him. "Don't be sorry for any of this," I say. "Today has been a *great* day."

Contributors

ROBB ASTOR grew up along Lake Michigan in the village of Pentwater. He served as a Peace Corps Volunteer in the United Republic of Tanzania. Robb lives in Traverse City, Michigan. His collection of poetry, *Bitter Dagaa*, was selected for publication by Michigan Writers Cooperative Press in 2014. A number of his poems have been published in the *Dunes Review*. Many things inform Robb's poetry— the natural spaces of Northern Michigan, astronomy, but mostly the daily wonder of encountering beauty in the strangest of things.

GRETA BOLGER is a poet and visual artist living in her Aunt Beulah's old house in Benzonia. Her writing has been published in several online and print journals, and she just recently sold her first pieces of visual art. She has learned that the "After" never ends, but it can, in time, be made into things of beauty and comfort. This is what she chooses to do.

JULIA BRABENEC has lived in Leelanau County since 1975 when she and her husband came to settle in the area they had loved since discovering it on their Honeymoon in 1948. Some of the land they purchased became the site of an organic orchard of peaches and apples which they tended together until John's death in 2010. Northport has become their Everlasting Home.

ROSEMARIE CANFIELD lives on a 40-acre farm in northwestern Michigan with her husband, two dogs, two horses, and many other animals and gardens, because they raised their 9 children in an organic environment before organic was popular. She is a member of Michigan Writers and is currently working on a memoir.

LISA BURRIS is a Michigan State Spartan who holds a bachelor of science degree in social work. She exited the field to raise her three living children and is now a proud elementary school secretary in Petoskey, Michigan. Lisa loves reading, mountain and road biking, and hiking through deeply wooded forests. Lisa is a frequent contributor to *Michigan Bicyclist Magazine*, was a participant in the 2018 "Poet's Night Out" in Traverse City, Michigan, and was a contributing writer for the 2018 *Bay View Literary Magazine*. Lisa believes that loss was a gift she was lucky to receive early; she chooses to live a happy life.

ROO DAVISON is a writer interested mostly in economics and political economy, and is currently working on a book on how to fix American politics. He has a degree in Engineering from Leicester University, and an m.sc. in Computer Science from Imperial College, London. He is also a graduate of the guitar program at the Atlanta Institute of Music. When not writing, he works with his wife, Ellie Harold, running an art gallery out of their home in Frankfort, Michigan.

AMANDA FORRESTER began writing poetry as an outlet for grief after losing her son to suicide in 2012. She participates in Writing Through Loss at Michael's Place, where she feels accepted and understood. Amanda finds comfort in her faith and the love of family. Her greatest pleasure is being Nana to her ten grandchildren.

MELISSA FOURNIER, lmsw, works as the Program Director for Michael's Place, a non-profit bereavement support center in Traverse City, MI, where she facilitates Writing Through Loss, an ongoing writing program exploring and supporting the grief journey. Melissa has worked in adult, pediatric, and perinatal hospice, as well as mental health and has been a featured speaker on end-of-life, perinatal loss, and loss by suicide. She holds an msw from the University of Michigan and a ba in Psychology from Wayne State University. She is currently a student of Narrative Medicine with Columbia University's School of Professional Studies. Her writing has appeared in *Dunes Review, The Sow's Ear Poetry Review, Pulse: Voices from the Heart of Medicine,* and *Medical Literary Messenger.* She is the author of *Abruptio* (The Poetry Box, 2019), a chapbook of poems honoring the life and death of her daughter born prematurely.

ANGELA KNAUER HAASE earned her mfa from Vermont College of Fine Arts and her undergraduate degree from Western Michigan University. She is a native of Benzie County. Her poems have appeared in *Mississippi Review* and other journals and were included in *Poetry in Michigan, Michigan in Poetry,* from New Issues Press, 2013. Mayapple Press holds two titles by her—*With A Cherry on Top* and *Live From the Tiki Lounge.* She has finally found true love and the right work in her life—two miracles we should all be so fortunate to discover.

ALISON HARTMAN resides in Baltimore, Maryland. She has an MFA from Yale University and previously taught sculpture at the Rhode Island School of Design. She is an acupuncturist and has maintained a private practice for 34 years. "Mending" was written one year after her son's unintentional heroin overdose in 2017. Together with her son's physician, Dr. Shapir Rosenberg, she also co-wrote a performance piece on compassionate caregiving and bereavement which was presented at medical humanities conferences in the U.S. and Canada.

KATHRYN HOLL, MA, LPC, is the Grief Support Services Manager at Hospice of Michigan and an active member of the Association of Death Education and Counseling. Kathryn provides counseling, professional educational workshops and memorial services. She co-facilitates Writing Through Loss, a poetry and writing program for bereaved individuals offered at Michael's Place, and she has taught life writing at Northwestern Michigan College. Her passion lies in bringing grief and death discussions out into the open air of reality.

MARY ANNA KRUCH is a career educator and full-time writer, inspired by family, nature, and place. She leads a monthly writing workshop, Williamston Community Writers, and has written a textbook, *Tend Your Garden: Nurturing Motivation in Young Adolescent Writing*, along with several professional papers. Currently, she supervises student teachers part-time at a state university. Her poetry has appeared in *The Remembered Arts Journal*, *River Poet's Journal*, *Edition 3*, and *Plum Tree Tavern*. Her first poetry collection, *We Draw Breath from the Same Sky*, is in press. Mary Anna is married and has two grown daughters, a son-in-law, and a darling grandson.

ELAINE MCINTOSH is a retired nurse practitioner trying to live peaceably with the bears, foxes, owls living in the woods with her in Fife Lake Michigan. She has had her poems published in *Huron River Review*, *Dunes Review*, and *Bear River Review*.

SUSAN ODGERS has worn many different hats in the field of mental health, including teaching psychology at Northwestern Michigan College for the past 30 years. Since 2008, her column, "Adapted in TC," has appeared in the *Traverse City Record-Eagle*. Parts of this piece originally appeared in the *Traverse City Record-Eagle* in October 2009. In 2010, the Traverse City Human Rights Commission awarded Susan the Sara Hardy Humanitarian of the Year award. A 2017 Ragdale fellow, Susan was awarded another Ragdale fellowship for 2019. She is a member of several area boards and councils, including Michigan Writers, and co-hosts the monthly series "Poets Meet Musicians."

ANNE-MARIE OOMEN is author of *The Lake Michigan Mermaid* with Linda Nemec Foster; *Love, Sex and 4-H* (Next Generation Indie Award for Memoir); *Pulling Down the Barn* (Michigan Notable Book); and *Uncoded Woman* (poetry), among others. She teaches at Solstice MFA at Pine Manor College (MA), Interlochen's College of Creative Arts (MI), and at conferences throughout the country.

PENNY PARKIN, LCSW, practiced clinical social work in the Philadelphia area for more than 25 years before moving to northwestern Michigan. Her son Spencer died at age 21 from a congenital heart condition in 2008. "Heroes" is excerpted from her memoir, *Dance This Mess Around*. She lives with her husband and dog on Crystal Lake.

NORA LIU ROBINSON grew up in Northern Michigan as the daughter of a Chinese refugee and the great-granddaughter of a Finnish immigrant. Surrounded by a mix of cultures, she was struck by the importance of language and how it can either open doors or close them. Nora now teaches English to speakers of other languages at the Interlochen Arts Academy, and she has co-authored several articles in the *English Journal*, a journal for secondary English teachers. She lives in Traverse City, Michigan, with her family, including Charlie Sheen, the cat she inherited from her father.

MELISSA SEITZ lives along the western shoreline of Higgins Lake, Michigan, with her husband. Her writing has appeared in *The Bear River Review, The Dunes Review, The Lake, The Prose-Poem Project*, the *Walloon Writers Review*, and various other journals. Her photography has been published in the *Walloon Writers Review* and *Midwestern Gothic* (online version). Read her blog for essays on life, music, and travel at lifeirruption.com.

DANIEL STEWART is a writer, writing coach, editor, book designer and storyteller. He holds a PH.D. in history and writes memoir, personal essay and fiction (as well as the occasional eviction notice, because life is strange). He is the founder of History By Design, is a past president of Michigan Writers, Inc., and lives on an old farmstead in Leelanau County, Michigan, with his wife and a number of animals, some of them invited.

DIANA STOVER is an ordained minister who served churches in Ohio, Indiana, and Michigan before concluding her professional career as a hospice chaplain with Beaumont Health Systems. After her husband's death, she retired to spend time traveling, volunteering, writing and celebrating family. She and her son, Jacob, and his partner, Evan, are rehabbing a home in Detroit. She spends winters in Royal Oak and summers in Northport.

KIRK WESTPHAL is a water resource planner by day, and a writer by night. He has published poems in various journals, and recently published two books. His first book, *No Ordinary Game* (DownEast Books, 2015), is a collection of inspirational stories about great moments in sports that happen to everyday people. His second book is a collection of poetry entitled *Bodies of Wood and Water* (Kelsay Books / Aldrich Press, 2018). He is inspired by forests and rivers that remind us how to speak to one another.

Made in the
USA
Middletown, DE